Y0-BGG-131

MARRIAGE

Much More Than a Dream

REX A.
SKIDMORE

MARRIAGE

Much More Than a Dream

Deseret Book Company
Salt Lake City, Utah
1979

© 1979 Rex A. Skidmore
Printed in the United States of America
All rights reserved

Library of Congress Cataloging in Publication Data

Skidmore, Rex Austin, 1914-
  Marriage.

  Includes index.
  1. Marriage—United States. I. Title.
HQ734.S657   301.42'0973   79-26375
ISBN 0-87747-783-3

Contents

The Quest Begins — 1

Your Expectations — 5

Feelings Make the Difference — 9

Genuine Communication — 14

Loving — 19

Who Are You? — 27

Giving and Getting — 31

No Marriage Is Perfect — 35

Admitting Your Mistakes — 39

When Conflicts Arise — 42

Marriage Can Be Fun — 46

Teaming — 50

Opening Doors Through Appreciation — 55

Building, Not Bruising — 58

Dollars and Sense — 61

Trust Builds Trust — 65

Spiritual Values — 68

Parenting   72

Counseling Resources   78

Looking Ahead   83

Index   88

The Quest Begins

Getting married is exciting; staying married is not so easy.

Each year more than two million couples say "I do" in an aura of excitement and anticipation that "here is the ultimate in living." Each day Joes and Marys and Phils and Jeannes go to the marriage altar with love in their hearts and faith in their shared destiny. Nearly sixty million American families affirm the vitality of marriage, affirm the fact that more close ties inhere in family life than in any other social dimension.

Most persons who marry are dreaming of pink clouds of romance and ecstasy. Dreaming about marriage is all right, *if* the dreams are translated into realities. The challenge is to work with what is underneath the silver-lined clouds: the daily footsteps on the ground.

Wanting or expecting a successful marriage does not insure a successful marriage. Although marriage is more popular than ever before, more than a million marriages disintegrate in divorce each year in the United States. A century ago divorce was practically unheard of. Today it is a common event, so common that nearly twenty percent of the American population have walked away from wrecked marriages.

More than three thousand times every day, somewhere in the United States a judge's gavel comes down with a thump, and the courtroom walls echo the words "divorce granted"—dreams and expectations shattered.

A glimpse at one marriage indicates the need for help.

Diane and Craig went into their marriage sharing romantic dreams, filled with star-studded hopes and anticipations. They had a lovely ceremony, attended by caring relatives and close friends. Their three-day honeymoon at a seaside resort was fun and dreamy except for two difficult arguments about making decisions.

2

Two weeks after their blissful wedding, they were eating Sunday dinner at the home of Diane's parents. An argument arose between the young couple and soon the barbs were hurtful and intense. Finally Diane jumped to her feet in anger, bolted out the front door, jumped into their car, and drove away with a lurch. Craig, at first undecided as to what to do, soon started another car and went after his young wife. The newspaper account said Diane was traveling at nearly a hundred miles an hour when her automobile failed to make a curve, went out of control into the barrow pit, plowed through the sagebrush, and turned over three times. She was dead by the time Craig caught up with her.

Could this tragic episode have been prevented? The answer is probably yes—if more realistic preparation for involvement in marriage had taken place.

Again, getting married is exciting and relatively easy; building a meaningful marriage is an awesome challenge. Positive anticipation does not guarantee successful marriage. Most young couples go into marriage thinking their dreams will be fulfilled automatically: life will now be complete. They soon find out that living together, while wonderful in many ways, is more complicated than being single. Marriage brings individual needs and desires to the fore and bares conflicts and differences that were submerged under the romantic waves of courtship. Living together can add intimate, meaningful, and satisfying experiences to life, but it can also bring pressures, differences, and problems that have never been seen or felt before.

As a couple start along the trail of marriage, according to Dr. Paul Popenoe, it is well for them to keep in mind that "marriage is not a destination—it is a journey." A beautiful wedding, impressive and sacred in every regard, is not the culmination of life's ambitions; it is just the beginning or launching of an experience that may bring joy and happiness or emotional turmoil and heartache. It is the beginning of a life of new experiences, day in and day out, that are seldom the same and that bring satisfactions and challenges as the weeks go by. Marriage is not something that happens and takes care of itself. It is ever changing and ever growing.

Sociology professor Carl Kelsey suggests that "marriage is a process, not an event." The wedding ceremony opens doors to a life of give and take, of joy and sorrow, of challenge and ease, of pleasure and pain. Marriage is not an institution for children; it is for grownups, and requires maturity and giving as long as two people live together, and longer. It is something that takes daily effort, compromise, sharing, understanding, cooperation, and loving.

As couples move into marriage, they need to keep in mind three things: their attitudes, their thoughts, and their actions. They need to be aware of what they know, feel, and do. Most couples enter marriage with an abiding confidence that they know what marriage is all about and they have the requisite answers for a good marriage, even a wonderful marriage. They have heard about marriage, they have talked about marriage, and they think they know the paths to follow. They find after the wedding that although they understand much about marriage, in many ways they are just beginning to know what it is all about. Couples learn what marriage really is after the ceremony. Knowledge, in and of itself, is not enough; knowing about the principles of successful marriage will not automatically guarantee such a marriage.

Attitudes and feelings are extremely important. If a couple feel that marriage is for them, and they share positive emotions, they have taken a big step in the right direction. If they have a surplus of negative feelings and doubts, they are in for trouble. For most people, feelings control behavior more than thoughts or knowledge do. A positive attitude of faith and caring may help a marriage fulfill the dreams of both husband and wife.

Doing is most important of all. Couples may have adequate knowledge and even positive feelings, but if they stand by motionless, doing nothing, their marriage may

4

disintegrate before their very eyes. Successful marriage comes from putting into action what is known and felt. Thinking, feeling, and doing are all important, but doing is most important of all. It can ensure an atmosphere of love and provide an emotional climate for solving problems, building meaningful relationships, and deepening joy. It isn't what people think about or feel that makes the difference; it is what they do. For most, marriage is the greatest opportunity they'll ever have to put into action their personal ideas and feelings for the benefit of themselves, their mates, and others. A positive team of husband and wife can achieve meaningful contributions and accomplishments above and beyond what each could ever do alone.

Jeff and Ann, married nearly ten years, celebrated their anniversary by taking a hike. Both loved to roam the mountains and enjoy the beauties of nature. They arranged their anniversary "date" so they arrived at the top of a mountain ridge just as the sun was sinking in the west. They had enjoyed a leisurely walk along the trail, hand in hand, observing the flowers, the trees, and the rocks, and had even caught a glimpse of a fawn as they approached a thicket of scrub oak. They felt particularly close to each other as they reminisced about their ten years together.

The view to the west was magnificient: the sky filled with hues of azure and pink, the sun like a ball of fire as it sank behind the mountains. The houses and buildings in the valley below looked like miniature toys in a sandbox. Automobiles scurried like ants going hither and yon.

Jeff took Ann in his arms and kissed her affectionately. "Ann, darling, you are everything to me," he said. "I love you with all my heart." Ann tenderly kissed his forehead and responded, "Jeff, you are a wonderful husband and father. I love you too." What were they saying to each other? That their dreams were coming true, that marriage had opened the doors to them, and that walking along the pathway of life, arm in arm, had been meaningful and wonderful. It is evident that they had combined their knowledge, their feelings, and their actions into a harmonious togetherness that could lead them to new heights ahead. You can do the same.

Your Expectations

*J*im and Carol had been married three months. They were living in a one-room apartment while he attended graduate school. She was working as a secretary to support them financially. In their large apartment building, the residents took turns doing their laundry in the basement, using common facilities. One Saturday at noon, when Jim returned home from four hours of classwork, he entered the apartment thinking of food and found none—only a note saying: "Come see me, sweetheart. I'm downstairs doing the washing."

He sauntered downstairs. When his wife spotted him, she said casually, "Honey, why don't you help me finish the washing? Then we'll go upstairs and fix lunch together." The sparks flew. He retorted that there was no way he would help with the washing. She became upset and he left. Why had trouble developed over such a circumstance?

After awhile Jim returned and they talked through the whole situation. They then realized Carol had grown up in a home where her father often did the entire washing; Jim had been reared in a family where the mother would have run the father out of the house if he had even offered to help with the washing. When the differences in expectations were recognized, a compromise was made and a solution satisfactorily worked out.

Every husband and every wife goes into marriage with many ideas and expectations about what it is all about. Some of these ideas are realistic; others don't even come close. One newspaper described it this way: "A woman marries a man with the ridiculous idea that she can change him; a man marries a woman with the naive belief that she will continue to be the same."

Expectations are significant aspects of every marriage. Expectations relate to the self, the mate, and the marriage as a whole. Sometimes a mate will give his or her partner a map with many specific destinations and stopping places when the spouse hasn't planned a trip in that direction at all.

Every person comes to marriage with preconceived ideas about what to give and what to get. Each person usually expects to contribute much to a marriage and to receive much in return. Each person also has expectations for the mate, some things the mate should do and some he or she should not. When the couple's expectations are basically similar, harmony and satisfaction usually occur; when there is too much variance, difficulties often ensue.

Often a person's expectations of what he should give to marriage are too low, while his expectations of what he wants his partner to give are too high. The person who expects to give a minimum and get a maximum is due for some shocking awakenings. Successful marriage requires both partners to give and do much.

Too often husbands and wives seem to have tunnel vision when they get into real-life situations. They see only one point of view; they fail to empathize with their mates. On one occasion a marriage counselor was riding in his car with a friend who was having heartaches and problems in his marriage. The man bared his personal thoughts and feelings and was most critical of his wife, enumerating many things she did that he didn't like, and many things he liked that she didn't do. As they neared a mountain ridge with two peaks, the driver asked his friend which of the peaks was higher. The friend replied quickly, "The one to the south, of course." When they had driven a little farther, the counselor repeated the question. This time the reply was, "They look about the same." When the riders could look back, a few miles farther along the highway, the driver asked again, "Which looks higher now?" The friend replied, "The one to the north, of course. Which peak is, and why do you ask?" He had hardly finished posing the questions when he smiled and said, "I get it: what I see in my marriage and expect has much to do with where I am standing and where I am looking." Often couples look at the same marriage—theirs—and each sees things that are not present to the other. Yet each acts in accordance with what he thinks he sees.

Differences in expectations may be solved by couples who are willing to share their thoughts, questions, and doubts. Some helpful actions are:

1. Share often thoughts about what is expected of self, of each other, and of the marriage.

2. Realize that similar expectations can usually bring enhancement and reaffirmation of marital goals.

3. When serious differences exist and it is evident there is a need to talk them over, try to understand them, discuss them, and work out appropriate solutions—solutions with which each partner feels comfortable and satisfied. Ordinarily, this brings acceptable compromises. If not, if the differences still persist, a visit to a qualified marriage counselor may be the next step.

Sometimes spouses, individually or together, expect too much from their marriage. No marriage is perfect, or even close to it. Every marriage has problems and difficulties, because every marriage involves two imperfect individuals. Couples may strive for perfection and move onward, upward, and forward with their individual goals as well as with goals for their marriage, but if they expect or demand too much from each other they will soon be in trouble. Many marriages have broken up because one or both of the persons involved expected and demanded too much from the other. When the expectations are too high and unrealistic, failure is assured—and people can stand failure only so long before they pull out or run away to avoid untenable situations. Some couples are about as unrealistic in their expectations of marriage as the high jumper who says he is going to jump over the World Trade Center in New York City. If he makes an attempt, he'll bounce back from the foundation, an absolute failure.

It is desirable for couples to share and talk over basic goals and ideals in life, preferably before marriage, but soon after marriage if this has not been done before. Understanding what a person wants out of life is highly significant in the marriage relationship. A person who has money as his number one goal in life may run into real difficulty if his mate has little concern about finances as long as there is enough money for food, clothing, and shelter. The mate who wants to have a large family of seven or eight children is going to have problems if the spouse wants only one or two, or none. Basic ideals regarding gifts to churches or charity, recreational pursuits, educational goals, where to live, and how to socialize— these and many other ideas and values can make or break a marriage, depending on what each partner expects and on how flexible and understanding each is.

"As a man thinketh in his heart, so is he," is characteristic of the marriage endeavor. The more ideas, goals, and ideals that are tossed into the marital pool, the more opportunity the partners have for interesting experiences together. As expectations and goals are shared and discussed, maturity for both the mates is likely to develop along with happiness in the marriage.

Feelings Make the Difference

People usually marry because they want to be happy. Are you happy? Most of the time?

Feelings and attitudes in marriage are very important. How a person feels usually affects how he thinks and, in particular, what he does. Although happiness is a popular goal for marriage, it is unrealistic for persons to expect and demand complete happiness all of the time. Reality says that mates can be happy much of the time, but not all of the time.

Feelings have to do with emotions such as fear, anger, love, hate, anxiety, and depression. Feelings are powerful and often influence decisions more than rationality does. Husbands and wives act daily in accordance with their inner emotions—which may or may not be contrary to their best judgments.

Understanding one's own feelings and those of a mate is imperative to a successful marriage. It is essential to recognize that all people have both positive and negative feelings and moods, and feelings may change from moment to moment or from day to day. Some feelings are deep rooted and unexplainable; others are near the surface and can be readily detected and understood.

Marriage partners need to understand that both men and women vacillate up and down the emotional scale. In other words, no person can be "up" all the time. Mood swings are normal and, some say, desirable. Sensitive mates recognize emotional changes, accept them, and make allowances for them. Some couples may even devise signals to indicate to each other what is happening. These vary from couple to couple, depending on their respective temperaments. In the film *Who's Boss,* the husband twirled his hat on his finger as he entered the house if he had had a hard day at the office. This was a warning: "Don't pick on me tonight." If the wife had had a hectic day at home, she wore her apron astern, a signal to "take it easy with me." One couple agreed that, if a serious argument started to arise, the husband would go for a walk. Upon his return they would usually have cooled off enough to talk things over. Various other methods may be devised to handle differences that arise.

Husbands and wives who are sensitive to the feelings of each other try to discover what is really being felt, rather than what appears on the surface to be happening. It is easy to see marital mirages, which have no existence in fact. Some mates are like the man who, disheveled and exhausted, staggered across the dry, desolate desert. For two days he consumed neither food nor drink. Suddenly he thought he saw water ahead, and he began to run. Instead of reaching precious, lifesaving liquid, he kept seeing the water at a distance; consequently he put forth his last surge of energy in running and fell exhausted by the sagebrush. When searchers located his body several days later, they found he was within a mile of help. They concluded that if he had not seen the mirage but had pursued a steady course, he undoubtedly would have been rescued.

Every couple sees some mirages in marriage. All are influenced by misimpressions and misunderstandings—some more than others. Many marriages are pried apart because husbands and wives see things that are not there and fail to sense the real feelings that are present. For example, an upset wife may blast her husband with the words "I hate you," when what she is really trying to convey is that she loves him, but resents the fact he does not spend more time with her.

Couples need to share their feelings, both positive and negative, with their mates. Many spouses share only positive feelings, trying to impress each other or act superior. Everyone has negative feelings, and ordinarily if people bring them out they feel better. As couples share inner feelings, they are generally helped therapeutically, and the bond between them deepens. For example, Ted came home from work discouraged and unhappy. He had failed to make a sale he had been working on for three weeks. Liz let him talk about it, and before long he felt much better. In another home, while the family was eating supper Sally dropped a beautiful dish, a family heirloom, and began to cry. Her husband put his arm around her, listened to her outburst, and assuringly said, "That's all right, honey. We have lots of other keepsakes." She soon felt better.

Positive feelings usually inhere in achievement and successful activities; negative feelings often arise from failures and dissatisfaction. Sometimes competition between husband and wife introduces an unwarranted amount of negativism. Husbands and wives need to recognize that they will inevitably be in competition with each other at times, and they must learn to accept and handle negativism so its influence can be minimized.

Mature mates gain satisfaction vicariously through the skills and achievements of each other; they don't have to feel equal in everything, or superior. A sensitive wife gains personal satisfaction when her husband gives a good speech or makes a special achievement at work; she even feels positive when he cooks something better than she can. A mature husband, likewise, gains satisfaction from the achievements of his wife. Mature mates foster a team relationship, not a competing twosome. For example, they do not compete for the love of their children; they do everything they can to deepen the children's love for both of them, individually and together.

Sensitive mates who empathize with each other do two things: (1) listen to expressions to bring out the feelings of their mates, and (2) act supportively, building their mates rather than psychologically battering or bruising them. An approving, understanding mate can help dilute or eliminate questionable feelings.

In addition to helping dissolve or reduce negative feelings, partners may encourage and enrich the positive ones. Love deepens as couples express and respect their love for each other. Love increases as it is tapped and shared.

When husbands and wives admit the truth, they

generally acknowledge that there are things they both like and dislike about each other. The tendency often is to deny or hide the dislikes. No two persons are the same, which means that at times conflicts resulting from differences will arise. A couple need to keep in mind that it is all right to dislike something the husband or wife does. A person may even hate some activity of his or her spouse, but still realize that it is the act or behavior, not the person, that hurts. For example, a wife may hate the procrastinating nature of her husband while still loving him as a total person.

Anger is a common emotion that is often involved in tottering marriages. It varies in intensity and pervasiveness, but it needs to be understood and worked with. David and Vera Mace, world-renowned marriage counselors, suggest three steps in handling anger within the marriage arena: (1) recognize that anger is normal, (2) try to understand what it is all about, and (3) help each other to overcome the anger. If couples recognize and accept the normalcy of anger in marriage, they are well along the way to handling it. It is impossible for any two persons to live together without some differences arising, bringing conflicts. With conflicts come some resentments and anger. Mature couples will realize that anger is normal at times in marriage and will learn to deal with it in a productive manner.

The second step is to talk over the conflicts and try to understand what brought about the anger. Sometimes the answer is simple, sometimes complex. The anger may have been caused by an innocuous misunderstanding in communication. For example, a couple decided to send a condolence to the home of a bereaved friend. The husband called the florist on the telephone and started to order a plant; the wife interrupted and said, "Get a planter." He ordered the planter, but was angry because she had commanded him. When they talked it over after he hung up the telephone, they realized they had not communicated well in the first place. He had had in mind a plant and she a planter. Other problems may be more complex, but if there is a sincere attempt to understand the anger, a solution will likely evolve.

The last step is to help each other change the situation so that in the future anger is minimized or eliminated. In the above-mentioned illustration, the husband and wife agreed to improve their communication pattern by repeating back to each other the decisions and plans they would make. If both husband and wife are willing to work together to prevent or reduce anger-producing situations, they just about have it made. A mate who asks for help is seldom turned down.

A sense of humor—a valuable lubricant for handling many negative feelings—may turn conflict situations into fun situations. For example, one young couple had the wife's mother staying with them for a few days. The wife made some ice cream in a tray in the freezer compartment of the refrigerator. The husband came home from work, pulled out the tray, and said to his wife and mother-in-law, who were seated on the sofa in the front room, "Here, have some ice cream." In jest he pretended to throw the tray to them. Somehow the refrigerator plug had been pulled and the ice cream mixture hadn't set, so it sailed through the air, landing on the two on the sofa, on the carpet, and on everything else in between. Momentarily there was dead silence. Then all three began to laugh. They couldn't stop laughing. Now they joke about throwing ice cream.

In one sense, each husband or wife is a delicate instrument, a composite of tender feelings, which may produce beautiful music or discordant noise, depending on how tightly the instrument is drawn and also on the deftness and skill of the musician. The skillful musician knows how best to play the instrument to bring forth the desired result. He may realize it needs to be tuned and retuned before it will produce melodic sounds. Somewhat similarly, a wise husband or wife, sensitive to the orchestration of feelings in his or her mate, knows when to leave the partner entirely alone, when to love, when to talk, when to listen, or when to walk out of the room.

Genuine Communication

The inability to communicate between husband and wife and/or parents and children is a major problem. Some counselors say it is the greatest problem in marriage today. Again, no couple can communicate effectively one hundred percent of the time, but the more effectively partners can share ideas and feelings, the better their marriage is likely to be. Sir Isaac Newton observed that "men build too many walls and not enough bridges."

Clear communication is a decided asset for the marital venture. It tends to solidify and strengthen and is a resource for building relationships. Without genuine communication, all kinds of difficulties develop. The wife who says, "My husband hasn't told me he loves me in ten years. I'd give anything if he would," has a problem in dealing with him. More significantly, if he has not demonstrated his love to her, the marriage is in serious difficulty. Obviously, the lines of communication have failed along the way. What can be done to facilitate communication between husband and wife?

Communication can perhaps best be understood by looking at its two parts, sending and receiving, and some of the static or blockings that occur. Messages that people send or receive include ideas, decisions, or information, as well as such feelings as love, fear, anxiety, approval, or disapproval. Often a message is a combination of ideas and feelings forged together. For communication to be effective, it is imperative that the messages to be conveyed are clear in the mind of the sender; otherwise static may develop.

Sending a message involves verbal and nonverbal components. Verbal components are spoken or written words and can include both ideas and feelings. Sending may be done at different times and places, each of which may affect the results. To communicate properly, the sending should include enough sound, light, and feeling to convey specific messages or impressions.

Nonverbal communication is often more significant than verbal. It has to do with body movements and expressions, even including inflections of the voice. A particular stance may be part of the sending, along with tears in the eye, a shaky glance, a slouched position. The power of nonverbal signals is illustrated by the three-year-old girl who stepped from a car on the curbside and passed a mother with two children as she and her grandfather entered the yard. Little Julie said to her grandfather, "They don't like me." He asked, "How do you know?" She responded, "They had angry faces." Words do not need to be voiced in order for communication to take place. A nod of the head or a smile can convey all sorts of meanings.

Sometimes the verbal and nonverbal elements of a given communication do not coincide. For example, a wife may tell her husband, with whom she has been having difficulties, "I *really* love you." But the inflection in her voice conveys the opposite to him.

Some nonverbal signs stem from the unconscious mind, and they can be difficult to understand. They arise from the part of the emotional iceberg that is submerged in the water, yet may still influence the direction and flow of what is above the waves.

Many husbands and wives listen only on the verbal level of communication and don't even come close to getting the real message being sent. Understanding the importance of both verbal and nonverbal expressions is essential for effective communication. It is important for mates to listen with their hearts and their eyes as well as with their ears.

In effective communication, husbands and wives try to talk *with* each other rather than *to* or *at* each other. No one likes to be treated like a slave or a servant, especially not a wife or a husband. Talking with a mate on an equal level makes the flow of information and feelings a two-way process and facilitates communication. Dictatorship and an "I'm always right" attitude blast big holes and gaps in the road of talking things over. Definite, final opinions usually cause trouble. It is preferable to say, "It seems to me this is the way it is, but I'm not sure. What do you think?" Many people hesitate to express their ideas and feelings if an authoritative, all-knowing attitude saturates the conversational atmosphere.

Many husbands and wives attack or hurt each other as they attempt to communicate. Hurtful communication involves such phrases as: "You said . . . now don't deny it"; "You don't know what you're talking about"; "I'm right, you're absolutely wrong"; "Aw, shut your mouth"; "You idiot." Positive ways of questioning and even disagreeing include such phrases as: "I'm not sure, but it seems to me. . ."; "I'm uncertain—what's your opinion?"; "I may be wrong and often am . . ."; "One possible way is . . ."; "I don't quite understand your point, but help me to understand." The genius of communication is the art of asking, not of giving orders or blasting.

Clarity and completeness are vital factors in communication. A message should ordinarily be concrete, correct, and concise. It should also cover all the ground that needs to be shared; otherwise only part of the message can be received.

Receiving the message accurately is as important as sending it correctly. Mates should not only hear what is being said or evidenced nonverbally, but should really listen to the signals that are being transmitted. Listening involves much more than hearing. If communication is really to take place between husband and wife, it is absolutely necessary for ideas and feelings to flow in two directions; this requires both to be good listeners. The receiver should share the same ideas or feelings that the sender has transmitted: the closer they are to each other, the more effective the communication.

Keeping confidences is essential. Many experiences and ideas shared between husband and wife should not go beyond the privacy of the twosome. As mates honor the trust and confidence placed in them by their spouses, those spouses feel more at home in confiding further. On the other hand, if a wife begins to gossip in the neighborhood or to her club circle about confidential matters her husband has shared with her, he will strongly resent it; he will not likely share other matters again. Similarly, if a husband tells a friend something his wife has shared in confidence, the communication bridge between them is damaged.

Two additional steps are essential: getting feedback and handling differences regarding messages, if they exist. Feedback helps to ensure that both persons understand the same message. Every day people "hear" signals but get wrong messages, and trouble ensues. Obtaining adequate feedback, a simple process, can eliminate all kinds of problems. When the husband says, "I'll meet you at four o'clock on the corner of Capitol and Browning streets," the wife can respond, "O.K. I'll meet you on the corner of Capitol and Browning at four o'clock, right?" Communication often falls apart because one or both partners assume that what has been said has been heard.

If a message brings distress or differences of opinion, those involved need to carefully consider the issues and resolve them. A later chapter discusses this process. One communication resource is for husbands and wives to use each other as confidants, sharing both successes and failures. All people need someone to talk to on a confidential basis; ordinarily, mates can be very helpful in this regard. The cathartic value of sharing confidences has been described with an analogy by Joshua Liebman, in his book *Peace of Mind* (New York: Simon and Schuster, 1946, p. 37.) He explains that if you put a flame under a teakettle and keep the lid and cap on, sooner or later the teakettle will explode and possibly blow up the whole kitchen. However, if the cap is taken off the spout and some air is allowed to escape, the pressure is reduced immediately— some teakettles even begin to whistle. Similarly, people who release their pent-up feelings gain relief.

All people have feelings that well up within, and if they can open the valve so those feelings can vaporize a bit, many of the feelings disappear or are reduced in intensity.

Sharing of negative feelings, in confidence, can deepen the bond between man and wife in addition to being therapeutically sound. We all need outlets for verbalizing fears and anxieties.

The famous Old Faithful Geyser in Yellowstone National Park periodically builds up pressures and begins to rumble. About every sixty minutes an eruption takes place. Steaming water and vapors are shot into the still air through an opening in the cone. Within a few minutes the pressure is relieved and quietness returns. This is similar to what happens as husband and wife share anxieties, hostilities, disappointments, and fears that ferment and build up within. Psychiatrists explain that talking things out definitely makes sense. Recently a noted doctor pointed out that one reason women live longer than men is because they talk more. They are able to give vent to their feelings, which improves mental health and adjustment to life.

John Powell, a communications expert, says that "the genius of communication is the ability to be both totally honest and totally kind at the same time." Husbands and wives who accept these guidelines and put them into operation are more likely to communicate and build relationships in a positive manner. If dishonesty exists, sooner or later the lies surface; if kindness is not present, persons get battered and even psychologically butchered at times. This does not mean that mates always have to agree; in fact, often they will not. But it does mean they will use the best methods available to facilitate understanding of a situation and the action needed.

Loving

What is the most important thing in the world to you? How about to teenagers? To senior citizens? Joe Johns, age seventeen, replied, "I want to get married and be loved." Mary Smith, sixty-five, answered, "I've been married forty-four years. My husband and I love each other dearly. My greatest experience is to love my husband and have him hold me and love me." As the wooden paddle on the kitchen wall says, "Love is only for the young, the middle-aged, and the old."

Scientific studies show that the need for loving and caring is fundamental to living. Even the octogenarian whose husband had been dead fourteen years reminisced that their love had been the greatest experience in her life and was still sustaining her.

What is love? Every person has his or her own definition and explanation of what it is all about. Antoine de Saint-Exupéry said that "love does not consist in gazing at each other, but in looking outward together in the same direction." Psychiatrist Harry S. Sullivan explains that "when the satisfaction or the security of another person becomes as significant to one as is one's own satisfaction or security, then the state of love exists."

Love within marital and family circles embodies feelings that are positive and caring. Love is an endearment between two persons that brings joy and satisfaction. It is a positive emotion that exists when persons genuinely care about each other and consequently treat each other differently than they ordinarily would. It encompasses affection and togetherness, a sense of shared destiny, and mutual trust.

Marriage offers the greatest potential for loving and caring of any experience known to man. To realize as you drop off to sleep at night that the person next to you wants you, needs you, and cares for you is ever so important. Caring and loving are the heart of human relationships.

Dr. Abraham Stone, renowned marriage counselor, advises: "Mature love differs from childish love in that it desires not merely the satisfaction of self, of one's own needs, but even more the satisfactions of the mate. A couple maturely in love genuinely 'care' for one another. They want to establish a kinship of body and feeling. They do not romantically endow each other with illusionary qualities, but see and accept in one another both the virtues and faults." ("Before Young People Marry," *Reader's Digest,* September 1955, p. 40.)

F. Alexander Magoun, in *Love and Marriage,* explains the meaning of genuine love: "Love is the passionate and abiding desire on the part of two or more people to produce together the conditions under which each can be and spontaneously express his real self; to produce together an intellectual soil and an emotional climate in which each can flourish, far superior to what either could achieve alone." (New York: Harper and Brothers, 1948, p. 4.)

An absolute dichotomy between being in love and not being in love does not exist. Rather a continuum is present, and most couples find themselves in the middle area rather than part of either extreme.

Every husband-wife relationship provides the opportunity for deepening feelings of love, or for going in the opposite direction. A dynamic, growing love requires nutriment, not inaction or blind expectations. Love requires effort and use, and may well wilt on the vine if left alone.

Love is constantly changing, week in and week out. Joe and Lucille told their friends that when they were married they were sure they were in love. Five years later they indicated their love was much deeper, and after twenty years of marriage, they said with a chuckle, "When we were married, we didn't know what love really was. Now we do—it is great!"

Love is seldom static; it is generally either increasing or decreasing. It is a situation, says F. Alexander Magoun, "where two partners think more of the partnership than they do of themselves. It is an interweaving of interests and a facing of sacrifice together for the sake of both, for love is not love unless it is expressed in action. It is the feeling of security and contentment that comes with the adequate satisfaction of each person's emotional needs through their mutual efforts. It is man's superlative method of self-realization and survival." (*Love and Marriage, op. cit.,* p. 5.)

Dr. Smiley Blanton, in *Love or Perish,* explains that *"the flux of love*—the oscillation between attraction and repulsion—*is a normal part of every marriage.* True love between two people does not mean that one must become completely absorbed in the other. . . . The wise husband and wife know that even the deepest love must have its intervals of nonactive expression." (New York: Simon and Schuster, 1956, pp. 76-77.)

Most couples face basic questions: How do we maintain our love? How can we make it blossom even more? Tender and meaningful loving involves many actions, which include the following in particular: (1) giving of yourself and of your time, (2) sacrificing for your mate, (3) showing affection, and (4) nourishing the marital relationship.

1. *Giving.* In one sense the essence of loving is giving—of oneself and of one's time. Persons who really love do not only *take* time to be with each other—they *make* time. In this fast-moving world, with its pressurized schedules and scientific wonders, it is often difficult to free our time for those we care for—but it can be done and is done by those who really love.

Giving of self is in some ways even more important than giving time. This kind of giving includes frequent sharing of thoughts, feelings, abilities, and activities with one's mate. It means that partners do not withhold their hopes, goals, and plans in life from each other.

These dreams are shared and used to enrich the marital union.

The husband who seldom spends time with his wife and children because he is "too busy" may be saying that other things are more important to him. Most people give priority to that which they really want to do.

2. *Sacrificing for others.* A major manifestation of loving is the willingness and desire to sacrifice for another. People who say they are in love, and then always want and demand their own way, are deceiving themselves. Genuinely loving persons are those who often put their own desires and wishes into the background for the fulfillment of the wishes and desires of others. The mother who cleans office buildings at night for twenty years to save money to put her children through college, the wife who forgoes buying dresses she wants to help provide money for her husband to invest in his struggling business, the husband who sells his one car so the family can buy a house or mobile home—these illustrate loving sacrifice.

Part of loving a person is doing things for and with that person. This sometimes requires sacrificing, giving up the things one wants in order to provide for the needs of another. A husband may attend a particular movie or concert, not because he wants to, but just because his wife desires very much to go.

A sociology professor whose wife was bedridden with a stroke arranged his schedule to start work at four A.M. so he could finish his preparation, research, and teaching responsibilities early and be with his wife each afternoon and evening. When asked why he did this, he replied, "I do it because I love her. If the roles were reversed, she would do the same for me."

Another example is that of a father-in-law who was sitting early one spring morning on the front porch of the family home, where he lived in a basement apartment. It was cool even though the sun was shining on him. His son-in-law asked why he didn't turn up the thermostat for the furnace in the house. He replied, "I didn't want the noise of the furnace starting up to awaken the family."

3. *Showing Affection.* Affection is wanted and sought by all people, and marriage provides a fertile field for giving and receiving it. Outside of marriage, values and cultures differ, but within the sanctity of the marriage bond, affection belongs as a resource and a beautiful ingredient that can keep the marital venture running smoothly.

Affection embodies physical and psychological components. Physical affection varies: a kiss, an embrace, a hug,
and the touch of a hand are all part of it. These endear-
ments can build a marriage and enrich it; they can revi-
talize and bring joy and satisfaction. Lovemaking, love's
personal witness between husband and wife, is intimate
and meaningful. It can be beautiful and reassuring, exhilarating and renewing.

Psychological affection is also essential. This includes
words of endearment, written messages of love, and other
activities that can help a marriage blossom. The husband
who says, "My wife has not told me she loves me for more
than a year" is hungering for a witness of caring. The husband who has not told his wife she is his "one and only"
during the past month is missing the boat. We all need to
hear, often, that we are lovable and wanted.

Between husband and wife, sexual relations, the most
intimate kind of affection, are a desirable resource. Although a major function of physical union may be for bear-
ing children, nevertheless it serves in other ways to bring
meaning to marriage. Husband and wife may attain a oneness physically that unites them in many ways. The sexual
relationship within marriage is a personal witness of the
love of two people who have promised their trust and help
to each other. As such it may strengthen the marriage,
bringing joy, security, and deep satisfaction.

Intimate physical affection should be engaged in when
mutually desirable. This means that both husband and
wife need to be sensitive to the delicate feelings and emotional moods of each other. The husband who forces his at-
tentions on his wife may gradually destroy her affection for
him. Sensitivity, patience, and understanding ensure satisfaction in the art of lovemaking.

Learning to adjust physically often takes time, just as
adjustment in other areas takes time. Many couples take
months, and some, years, to adjust satisfactorily to each
other. Others never get along very well; yet it is interesting
to note that most of these persons, according to research
studies, consider their marriages successful.

Following are a few ideas married couples might keep in
mind to help them get along better affectionately:

a. Courtesies and "the little things" do much to develop and maintain personal affection between husband and wife. The wife who says, "The only time my husband is interested in me is when we go to bed," is saying that her husband is a failure as a lover. He needs to be more attentive and romantic in regard to many of the little things that please her and in turn please him.

b. Men are more easily aroused than are women. This needs to be kept in mind in understanding the interests of each. At the same time the wife, when once aroused, stays that way longer than does the husband; the glow is slower to ebb away.

c. Simultaneous sexual climax is not so important as some persons claim. Psychiatrists and other experts indicate this is a goal to seek but one that has been overemphasized. Contentment that results from physical oneness, tenderness, and words of endearment is of utmost importance.

d. Some variety in show of affection between man and wife is desirable. Wise mates keep romance alive and nourish affection by special courtesies, surprises, and new ways of expressing their love. Mates who find contentment and affectionate satisfaction at home are not prone to go elsewhere for it.

e. Psychological preparation for lovemaking is important. There is need to initiate romantic overtures and use words of endearment to help prepare one's mate for intimate union.

f. Control is needed in marriage. Certainly a mature mate understands that physical affection is not appropriate at certain times: when either one is ill, during the latter part of pregnancy, soon after delivery, or when either partner is tired or depressed. Intimate affection should be used to build a marriage, not to enslave or destroy it. Resentment, rather than feelings of love, may surface if wisdom and sensitivity are brushed aside.

If a couple are not making satisfactory adjustment in intimate relations, there are several things they might do:

a. Both read a good book on the physical side of marriage. Oftentimes, the trouble is merely a lack of understanding and information.

b. Talk things over. The husband and wife who discuss their intimate feelings and problems have a good chance of working them through.

c. Consult a competent medical doctor. Talking with a doctor and getting a careful physical examination is helpful. This provides an excellent opportunity for asking personal questions and receiving accurate answers.

d. Go to another specialist. If the first steps do not bring the desired results, then the doctor may well encourage the couple to go to a specialist who may help with their particular problems—a marriage counselor, a psychiatrist, a gynecologist, or someone else.

Most couples are able to get along satisfactorily in their physical adjustment after they have been married for some time, especially if they maintain an understanding, patient, loving attitude toward each other. Affection is one of the most delicate and sensitive of all social experiences; it needs tender cultivation and use to grow and blossom. It also needs a warm, spontaneous attitude. Trying too hard may bring the opposite results from those desired, just as trying to force oneself to go to sleep may keep a person awake.

Affection within the bonds of matrimony is a wonderful resource for strengthening marriage and the family. It can bring warmth, romantic glow, and unity, welding husband and wife together.

4. *Nourishing the marital relationship* is an essential part of loving. With adequate nourishment the marriage may blossom profusely; without it, it may fade or die. President David O. McKay explained that "love, as the body, must have nourishment or it will starve. There is no great thing the man or woman can do to keep *love* alive and healthy, but there are many little things given daily, and, if possible, hourly—a kind word, a courteous act, a smile, an endearing term, a sparkle in the eye, an unexpected service, a birthday greeting, a remembering of the wedding anniversary—these and a hundred other seemingly insignificant deeds and expressions are the food upon which love thrives." (*Home Memories of President David O. McKay* [Deseret Book, 1956], p. 221.)

Mature husbands and wives understand that a marriage must be nourished if it is to be successful. For a tree to bear good fruit, the farmer must cultivate the soil, provide plant nourishment, supply adequate water, spray, prune, and care for it in numerous other ways. Somewhat similarly, a husband and wife need to cultivate and nourish their marriage; otherwise, it will fail to grow and may wither away. Leo Buscaglia, popular marriage counselor, suggests that the limitless potential of love within each person is "eager to be recognized, waiting to be developed, yearning to grow."

Who Are You?

Brad and Jennifer had been married nine years and had experienced an interesting, eventful life together. Four healthy children had been born into their home. Brad was a successful accountant, and both he and Jennifer felt they were getting along well. On the way home from work one day Brad was thinking about his marriage and his wife and decided she was probably tied to the home and the children too much. He decided to give her a day off for a change. When he arrived home, he said, "Honey, how would you like to take Saturday off and be on your own?" She nearly fainted on the spot, but finally replied that that would be great.

Saturday came and went with Brad holding down the fort. Jennifer went shopping, visited friends, and did other things of her choice. When she arrived home at the agreed-upon hour and entered the front door, the house was a shambles, with toys and clothes scattered all over. No one was in sight. She called for Brad. Soon he came to the front room, apparently exhausted, his hair flopped over his eyes. He said nothing, but handed her a piece of paper. (Mind you, he was a trained, meticulous accountant.) On the paper he had written:

Number of times gave children drink of water	17
Number of times changed diapers	5
Number of times straightened rooms	12
Number of times picked up toys	18
Number of times children asked permission to cross the street, the answer was "no"	10

Number of times children crossed the street	10
Number of times I'm going to do this again	0

28

For the first time in his life Brad realized what it meant to be a mother at home every day with four young children.

Understanding—or lack of it—is a major factor in marriage. Many problems arise and many marriages are dissolved because either or both mates fail to try to understand themselves, each other, and their marital constellation.

Understanding one's self is vital. Cervantes suggested, "Know thyself . . . for this is the most difficult lesson of life." How long has it been since you sat down with yourself and took a careful look at who you are, where you are, and where you are going? Every person, including you, is unique. Even your fingerprints cannot be duplicated by anyone anywhere. How accurate are you in understanding yourself and what you do, day in and day out? All persons harbor misconceptions about themselves, and all need to develop the ability to change when it will be in their best interest or in the best interests of those they associate with. Robert Burns penned the famous words: "Oh would some power the gift to give us, / To see ourselves as others see us! / It would from many a blunder free us."

An interesting and simple way to begin understanding yourself is to occasionally take a piece of paper, fold it lengthwise, and then write on one side: "What I like about myself." On the other side write: "What I dislike about myself." The challenge, obviously, is to increase the use of the positive attributes, and to reduce or minimize the negative. The person who thinks he or she is perfect is an impossible person to live with. On the other hand, mature persons are those who admit they make mistakes and then go on from there. When mates can admit mistakes and share their related feelings, they are well on the way to a successful and rewarding marriage.

Understanding the other person is equally important. Do you really know what your mate and children think and feel? Do you empathize with them often? This involves identifying with another person, particularly regarding emotions. How closely can you describe the inner feelings of your mate at a given moment? No one can do this a hundred percent of the time, but the closer a person can come, the better the situation. The more you know the ideas and the feelings of your mate, the more likely you are to reach wise and fair decisions. Many husbands and wives have little or no idea of what their mates really think and feel, and they make little or no attempt to find out. They are groping in the dark.

An Indian chieftain was called to Washington, D.C., to testify before a government committee. When someone asked his opinion of a friend, he stood up tall, in his colorful headdress and beaded buckskin clothes, and replied, "I can't give you an answer. I would not judge any person unless I had walked in his moccasins for at least two weeks." Do you really know what it would be like to stand in the moccasins of your spouse? If not, you need to find out.

All of us want to change others, especially those close to us. We think we have the answers to their lives. Experts agree, however, that the easiest person for one to change is oneself, not others. Husbands and wives who want to improve their marriages may well start by looking at themselves. Most people do not want to be made over by others. Research reflects that mates are most likely to change when their spouses accept them as they are.

It is important for couples to be realistic and view their marital situations clearly, not through rose-colored glasses. Oftentimes husbands and wives have inaccurate impressions of their relationships and situations, impressions not in keeping with facts. Yet each tends to act in accordance with what he thinks he sees. The closer mates come to the realities, the more likely their marriage is to be a success. This calls for husbands and wives to be open-minded at all times.

Tom was late for dinner by nearly an hour. When he entered the house, Susan jumped to conclusions and accused him of spending time with his pals. He retaliated by telling her off and remarking that her meal was "lousy." What were the facts? Tom had been called in to talk with his boss at the end of the work day, and Sue had had some troubles with the children that had limited her preparation of supper. When they finally were able to realize what had happened, the problems evaporated.

One wintry evening in the sprawling city of London an American traveler was caught in a thickening, pea-soup fog. The daylight began to disappear, and darkness gradually enveloped the humming metropolis. The vaporous air became heavy and thick and dark. Soon the traveler had to slow down his gait to a hesitant walk. He could feel or see nothing about him except the sidewalk under his feet as he edged along at a snail's pace. Soon he decided to stop walking altogether. He felt all alone in this huge cellar of utter darkness.

After a while he heard the slow swishing steps of another person who called out, "Hello, anybody around?" The two began to converse even though they could not see each other. What could they do? Where could they go? Suddenly the air cleared, temporarily, and the American tourist saw before him an English bobby in full uniform. They both observed they were standing under a street light, which was shining brightly. How different everything appeared when the policeman and the visitor saw and understood each other and their surroundings and knew where they might go for shelter and safety. Somewhat similarly, mature husbands and wives endeavor to find out and understand who each is and where at a given moment.

Giving
and Getting

Michelle, with glistening eyes and conviction in her voice, told Rebecca, "I want to get married, so I can be happy." Rebecca, who had been married for ten months, replied, "That's okay if you'll make your husband happy too." She explained that she was still excited about her marriage but had learned that living together with someone was more complicated than living alone, and that a successful marriage has to be built upon action, upon giving of self.

William Menninger, noted psychiatrist, suggests that the "essence of loving is giving, not getting." He explains that mature couples are able to give of themselves *to* and *for* each other and *to* and *for* the welfare of the marriage as a whole. Thousands of marriages terminate each year because one or both of the mates is reaching only for his or her happiness, and neglects, disregards, or cares little about the happiness of the mate.

Some writers are still advocating the "do your own thing" approach to marriage; most writers, counselors, and married persons disagree. Mature persons seek many things they want and need, but they help their mates do the same. After all, marriage is a social relationship involving two or more persons. Ignoring, blocking, or hurting other persons invariably backfires and damages relationships. Stated positively, the more spouses give to each other and to their marriage, the more likely they are to achieve the happiness they want in life, and the more the needs and wants of others will be fulfilled. Excessive getting in marriage may make a person selfish, egocentric, and damaging; giving, on the other hand, tends to bring sparkle, enrichment, constancy, and support.

The person who says, "I want to get married so I can be happy," is a poor risk for marriage; so is the spouse who says, "I want to get everything out of marriage I can, regardless of what it means to the mate." A selfish person makes an inadequate marriage partner. Mates need to minimize the use of "I" and "my" and replace them with "we" and "our."

Mature persons give of themselves to the marriage, not just partially, but totally. They share their thoughts and feelings, their goals, their wishes—and their problems too. They make themselves available for other persons when needed or wanted.

Steve and Sharon, wondering why they were having serious difficulties in their marriage, went to a counselor. It was soon evident what their trouble was. Each believed and practiced the idea that marriage is a 50-50 proposition, and each endeavored to operate on that premise. What actually happened was that each usually reached about 45 to 48 percent—which was not enough. They came close to meeting the needs and wishes of each other, but were just a little bit short. Two 48s add up to 96 percent—just short of 100 percent. What is needed is for husbands and wives both to give, as nearly as they can, 100 percent of themselves to their marriage. Two 100 percents add up to much more than is needed for the achievement desired. A half person or a three-quarters person is a poor risk in marriage.

Giving your total self to another involves an honest sharing of yourself as you are: physically, economically, socially, psychologically, and even spiritually. As couples really feel they belong completely to each other, it follows that they feel closer, more supportive, and even more tender during precious moments. A spirit and practice of giving can really lubricate the wheels of marriage and bring melodious mutuality.

The mature mate who wants a successful marriage gives not only himself but also his time—not all of it, but enough to fulfill the needs of himself and his marriage partner.

Today's world is a pressurized one in which time is at a premium. People often say, "I'd do this but I just don't have the time," or "Oh, how I wish I had the time to do this or that." Everyone has the same twenty-four hours a day, and there is no way these hours can be increased. However, all people waste time, and all make choices regarding priority in the use of it. People are usually kidding themselves when they say they don't have time for their husbands or wives or children.

Time management is gaining stature in business and other circles. It is becoming recognized that everyone can improve his use of time to make more time available. Studying suggestions and guidelines put out by time management experts can be of great value.

Another important factor is the selection of priorities. People usually can do what they really want to do, although there are exceptions. When a person says that he doesn't have time to do something for or with a mate, he often means that the matter really is not important to him—that he'd rather do something else. Husbands and wives who say and show that they don't have time for each other are usually saying, "You are not very important to me." "You are low on my list of priorities." "Other things are way ahead of you." Mature mates face, honestly, the question of priorities in marital relationships.

On the positive side, what is more flattering than for a mate to say, "I want to spend the next three hours with you," or the weekend, or two weeks? The husband who breaks away from his busy office to have lunch with his wife is showing her that she is important to him. And the wife who says, "It really doesn't matter where we go, just so we are together," is complimenting her husband in a very meaningful way.

Mature husbands and wives take time for their mates, and make time for them even though pressures mount. With rare exceptions, it is possible, through careful planning and setting of priorities, to work into one's schedule time for husband-wife companionship and activities together. At times mates need to say no to some requests that are less important than their marriage.

Another element in giving is the sharing of talents.

Every husband and wife has talents, some yet untapped, that can be used to build a marriage. For example, abilities in art, writing, music, and cooking can be used to benefit each other and a marriage. The husband who learns to cook can relieve his wife at times by sharing some of that responsibility. The wife who has the ability to write may help her husband edit some of his writings. People who are expert and capable in planning and setting objectives can help by sharing such abilities with their mates. Of course, care has to be taken so that personal talents are not forced on the spouse, but are available when wanted or needed.

The final component of giving lies in the financial realm. Wise husbands and wives share their economic assets as a team, yet have a bailiwick of their own with some funds available for individual plans and choices. In most homes the husband is still the main breadwinner, although forty percent of married women now work outside the home. A mature husband realizes that his income belongs to the whole family, and he shares it accordingly. If the wife provides the main support for the family, the same situation should apply. If they both work, their two incomes should belong to the whole family and be shared. Some husbands and wives think that what their spouse earns is for the family and what they earn is for themselves: "My earnings are mine and your earnings are ours." This usually causes conflicts and problems. The important thing to learn is that giving, not getting, is the essence of successful marriage. Sharing builds a marriage, helping it grow and blossom.

Happiness in marriage, according to President Spencer W. Kimball, "comes from giving, serving, sharing, sacrificing, and selflessness."

No Marriage
Is Perfect

*J*an liked movies; Ron did not. Prior to their wedding they went to a movie about once a week. After they were married Ron hesitated and stalled and they rarely went. Jan became upset and claimed that if Ron really loved her he'd accompany her to the movies. The sparks flew and battles started. Finally, the couple sat down and talked about their problem. They tried to understand each other and what each wanted.

Jan and Ron struggled to reach a compromise. Finally they agreed they would go together to a movie about once a month, and if Jan wanted to go more often, she would go with a girl friend. This sore spot disappeared. They had adjusted to each other, not changed each other. They had both accepted the fact that they differed on the movie situation, and had gone on from there. The practice of acceptance is fundamental in successful marriage. Fortunate are couples who can be genuinely accepting of each other; those who cannot are in trouble.

Acceptance means to recognize and be willing to get along with the person and situations as they are, not as we want them to be—and there is often a big difference. Mature husbands and wives receive each other as they are and have goals and ideas for improving themselves and each other as well as their marriage, but realize that the best way for both to grow is to be accepting of each other.

Some marriage partners act as judges, often condemning and criticizing their mates. They even pass sentences on their spouses at times, telling them what to do and what not to do. Marriage is a partnership that combines two equals into a team, not putting one above the other. Giving and helping, not judging, make a functional marital team. Freedom of choice and freedom of action are essential for a viable relationship.

Acceptance is essential in marriage because no person is perfect, or even close to it. Each brings to marriage all of his or her previous life experiences—everything he or she is. Every person possesses many limitations as well as assets, shortcomings as well as resources. These imperfections may be physical, psychological, social, or spiritual—or rooted in all four. Mature mates recognize that two imperfect individuals living together in the closeness of marriage are bound to have many differences. Sound, enduring relationships are built upon honest and total acceptance of these differences.

Wise mates understand that it is normal to have ambivalent feelings toward each other; hostile as well as positive emotions may appear at times on the horizon of everyday living. A wife may complain because her husband is not bringing more money home. A husband may feel there would be more money if his wife took better care of the clothing and the home. A wife may resent her husband's being late to dinner often, and a husband may be disturbed because his wife will not get out of bed before he goes to work in the morning. Most of the time successful couples have positive feelings toward each other, but at times opposite feelings arise. Mature people recognize that vacillation of feelings is normal and can be accepted without fighting back.

Changes can and do take place, but usually through interest and support rather than through pressures or dictatorship. A person should work to change himself first before trying to make his mate over.

An example of the power of acceptance is the following case of a drinking husband. Both he and his wife received counseling from a psychiatrist. She had been encouraged to accept and love her husband, to stop criticizing and condemning him. He had quit drinking two or three times, but then had gone back to the bottle again. On one occasion, when he had not had a drink for nearly three months, she asked him to go to the store and purchase a loaf of bread for supper. On the way he met a friend who invited him to "have a couple of beers." He resisted at first but then gave in. One drink led to another, and before long he was drunk. He did not return home for two days. When he finally walked in the front door, his wife greeted him with a kiss and casually asked, "Where is the bread?" He immediately went to the store, purchased a loaf of bread, and has never touched liquor since. This was total acceptance.

Another example of acceptance relates to relatives. When you marry, you marry the whole family, whether you know them or not. Invariably differences arise when the marital constellation comes into existence. In-laws always possess many expectations and hopes for their children and the spouses of their children—some realistic, some far from it.

Mature mates admit and understand that family ties are powerful, and that even though a couple may set up a kingdom unto themselves at the marriage altar, they are always part of their larger families, influenced by them directly and indirectly. Sometimes family influence is more powerful at two thousand miles' distance than when the couple live in the basement apartment of in-laws.

This does not mean that a couple are forced to follow the guidance and direction of relatives. They may well listen to them, try to understand what they are saying, weigh their situations carefully, and then make their own decisions. Accepting relatives as they are does not mean following their advice—it may or may not. Ultimate authority and decisions should rest with the couple. However, they often can benefit by listening to and interacting with those close to them who care. Relatives, drawing upon a variety of life experiences, can often make suggestions and provide information or skills that may be of practical help to a couple. For example, when a couple are ready to buy a house, in-laws who have bought houses may share practical suggestions that could save the couple thousands of dollars.

The challenge in marriage is to be accepting of each other as total persons with all the differences that exist. If the differences are small and of little consequence, why not just accept them? They may well add color and meaning to a marriage. If the differences are big and do make a difference, then an honest attempt should be made to talk them over, face them, and work out solutions.

If compromises cannot be made, two alternatives exist: to accept the differences as part of life and not let them bother you, or to seek professional counseling and help. Marriage and family counselors are available for consultation in most cities.

Mature mates do not let differences bother them, or at least they keep the concerns at a minimum. In other words, if your mate has a problem, it doesn't need to ruin you. Do everything you can to help, and then go about your own business. Each person needs to keep a movie-camera approach, sensing action as it happens, not behaving in accordance with a single stilted snapshot of the past.

Admitting
Your Mistakes

*E*veryone makes mistakes, in and out of marriage. Every husband and every wife makes frequent errors. Questions arise: What shall I do? Shall I admit the mistake? Deny it? Blame someone else? Cover up and lie? Answers to these questions make telling differences in marriage. One husband told his wife, "I think people should admit their mistakes. I would if I made any."

There are three main ways to handle mistakes: deny them or lie about them, blame them on someone else, or assume personal responsibility and admit them. Each path leads to a different destination—the first two toward a dissolution of a marriage, the last one to a mature relationship.

In one sense the easiest way to handle a mistake is to deny it and lie about it. The husband may say, "I didn't break the confidence," "I didn't cause the dent in the car," "I did mail the letters." Or the wife may say, "I didn't break the dish," "I didn't forget to invite the Harrises to dinner," "I did feed the cat." These are common occurrences between husbands and wives.

Although it seems easy at the time to tell little white lies, sooner or later this practice backfires. While it is intended that a lie will never be divulged, sooner or later it comes to the surface. Someone either forgets to keep a secret or wants to get even. John Dillinger was betrayed by one of his girlfriends as a retaliation for loss of his personal attention and affection.

Immature persons often blame their mates for things

that happen. "You made the baby cry." "You forgot to put out the dog." "You neglected to put gas in the car." "You made us late for the meeting." "You didn't keep what I told you to yourself." "You didn't get things ready for the trip." Oftentimes their accusations are projections of their own mistakes onto their spouses.

Putting blame on someone else for one's own misdeed is a mark of immaturity. It is a common behavior to try to build oneself up by tearing someone else down. Mature individuals do not berate or blame others as a cover-up for their own errors. A sound relationship cannot be built when a person ignores his own responsibilities or blames others for them.

The mature way to handle errors is to admit them. The mate who can say, "I made a mistake, I'm sorry," is well on the way to strengthening relationships. Mature persons endeavor to understand what the realities are and to allow for them. If an error has been made, they swallow their pride, admit their mistakes, and ask what can be done to rectify them.

The words "I'm sorry," when sincerely voiced, are among the most powerful used between husband and wife. Wise indeed are husbands and wives who use these often, who admit their errors and indicate they feel sorry. Charlie W. Shedd, popular author on marriage, suggests that apology is one of those places in marriage where "Who did it?" or "Why did he?" or "How could she?" isn't as important as "What is the quickest way of making things right again?"

Assuming responsibility for our own behavior means admitting what we do or don't do, and then going on from there. We don't blame others for our actions. Others can't do things to us unless we allow them to. Self-justification is not nearly as important as what the facts are and how we can proceed.

When John came home an hour late for dinner and his wife was angry, he responded, "I got busy at the office and couldn't call you." What actually happened was that he had visited a friend on the way home, and the visit had lasted longer than he expected. Within a few days the man he had visited commented to the wife something about their visit—and real trouble arose. If John had told the truth, he would have been better off then and later.

When Mary backed into a car while driving out of a parking lot, she dented the rear of her husband's car. Should she tell the truth? She did, and although he was upset, he took the matter in stride and accepted the accident. If she had lied, and he had found out later, what would have happened to their relationship?

Jim forgot to mail two letters for his wife. When the persons who failed to receive them called and complained, she asked Jim if he had put them in the mailbox. He admitted that he had been forgetful, and he apologized. Although this was a touchy situation, it ended much better than it would have had he tried to lie his way out. A husband and wife who are absolutely honest with each other, who assume responsibility for their own acts, and who admit their errors build and nurture a mature relationship. When the opposite takes place, relationships and marriages begin to totter.

Since all people make mistakes, some not so little, another factor comes into consideration—the need for forgiving. When a mate recognizes that he or she has made a mistake, and apologizes, a mature partner not only appreciates what has been said, but also says, "It won't bother me. Let's forget it," conveying a forgiving spirit. Even when major errors have been made, the best answer is to develop understanding and offer forgiveness. Since no one is perfect, the door should be open at all times for admitting wrongdoing, indicating sorrow for it, receiving forgiveness, wiping out the past, and, in particular, paving the way for a better future ahead.

When Conflicts Arise

*C*arla and Doug couldn't agree about who should take out the garbage. She felt this was a man's job, and he thought either or both could and should do it. One evening they began to argue and had a big fight. Finally Doug walked out the front door and did not return until two A.M. What was the trouble? What was the answer?

All marriages have conflicts, whether couples admit them or not. Some couples keep conflicts submerged so they are not visible, but they are still there. Most couples know they have conflicts and recognize the challenge to their marriages, sometimes culminating in separation or divorce.

Having conflicts in marriage is not usually serious—unless the couple cannot face them and handle them. In a museum at the University of Alaska in Fairbanks is a pair of entangled, interlocked moose horns. Apparently two animals died because they were in deathly conflict and could not extricate themselves. Marriages may die too, if difficult conflicts are not settled.

The first step in finding solutions to conflicts is to recognize that conflict in marriage is normal because of differences in personalities of people. Also, differing wants and needs invite different actions. Since it is impossible to go in two directions at the same time, frustrations and hurts arise, depending on the forces present and the directions taken. Just because there are differences doesn't mean you have to be disagreeable.

Some authorities indicate that conflict is not only normal in marriage, but also desirable. They suggest that conflicts can bring growth and enrichment in living. After all, we move ahead as we face problems and solve them. A Chinese proverb says, "Crisis means opportunity as well as danger." On the other hand, most people feel that conflicts that result in serious arguments, quarreling, and battles can damage marriages. Most feel that developing a pattern for handling conflicts when they do arise is essential for sound husband-wife relationships.

A genuine acceptance by both husband and wife that conflict is normal is usually enough to take care of minor differences. However, if deeper conflicts arise that begin to eat away the marriage, then there is need for positive action. Battles seldom solve problems; instead they bring losses to both persons. Many mates want to win arguments, to prove they are right and their partners are wrong. But seldom is there a clear-cut right and wrong. The basic question should be, "What is best?" An answer to this question usually takes understanding and work.

After recognizing the inevitability of conflict, the second step is for couples to talk things over. Oftentimes conflict arises from misunderstanding, and when the situation has been clarified, a problem no longer exists. If this happens, so much the better. If this does not take place, one person can often make a shift that will solve the problem, and both can feel good about it. If they have been quarreling over the time for dinner, maybe one or the other can make a simple change in scheduling to relieve the situation. If they fight over the one car, maybe an easy change in planning by the husband or the wife will provide the answer.

Another solution involves both mates doing some shifting. This might be done both in regard to the dinner hour mentioned above or the use of the car, or in relation to almost any differences that exist. When both partners change, there is usually a reaching of middle ground, the most frequently used kind of compromise for solving conflicts and differences.

Another important action is for mates to ask for assistance from each other in reducing conflicts between them. Rarely does a marital partner refuse such a request.

Henry Bowman suggests that "adjustment does not imply that one person shall change to suit the whims of the other, that one shall do all the adjusting, or that one shall be imposed upon by the other. It implies merely that on the basis of the understanding of difference those things be done that increase the mutual satisfaction of the persons concerned." (*Marriage for Moderns,* 6th ed. [New York: McGraw-Hill, 1970], p. 8.)

If the above actions do not bring desired results, the couple may seek outside help. They need to talk over the nature of their problems and then seek a qualified person who can be of assistance. If they cannot pinpoint their problems, then the best person to go to might be a general marriage counselor, one who is used to talking with persons about all kinds of personal and family problems. Such a counselor would likely either work directly with the couple or refer them to another person who might help with their particular problems.

Professional marriage counselors are available in most cities. Usually it is best to get referral recommendations from known professional persons, as there are many quacks who milk the public for millions of dollars annually. Worse than that, these unscrupulous persons often hurt couples and damage their marriages. Their aim is to get money into their pockets, not to provide competent services. Most doctors or lawyers are able to make referrals to competent marriage counselors. Or a community services council can offer a list of reputable local counselors.

Before couples go to marriage counselors it is helpful for them to know something about the counseling process. Marriage counselors usually do not tell people what to do, but help them to understand themselves better and to consider alternative plans of action. They do not prescribe simple psychological pills to dissolve the conflicts. They help persons to face their problems, to talk about them, and to utilize their own and other resources to bring about solutions. Most of the work has to be done by the persons with the problems. The counselor is a facilitator and an enabler who tries to help troubled people help themselves.

He helps people to consider both their thoughts and feelings—particularly their feelings.

Marriage counselors sometimes make referrals to other
experts, which action can be helpful. If a couple are
concerned about budgeting, consultation with a home
economist or financial consultant may pay big dividends. If
a couple are having difficulties in lovemaking, a visit to a
competent medical doctor or psychiatrist may bring
changes for the better. If they possess differing philoso-
phies and values, spiritual or otherwise, a visit to their
church leader may bring the desired results.

When a Latter-day Saint couple have a major conflict
in their marriage or family that they cannot resolve by
themselves, they are encouraged to make an appointment
with their bishop. The bishop, in confidence, can often help
a couple talk about and work through their differences. If
such problems persist, the bishop can make stake counseling resources available, provided by professionally trained
volunteers, or refer the couple to LDS Social Services for
assistance.

On the positive side, it should be kept in mind that
conflict can often be a challenge for growth. Many couples
have gone clear to the edge of the cliff of despair, at which
point they have really faced up to where they were and
where they really wanted to go. Millions of couples have
used differences and conflicts for growth, strengthening
their relationships. The basic question is not so much what
the problem is, but what those involved are willing to do
about it. Couples who maturely face differences and
conflicts usually come out on top, with increased wisdom
and deepened marital bonds.

Sometimes it takes only a little change to make a big
difference. A captain can alter the direction of his ship by
a mere touch of the hand on the helm. A tiny rudder on a
big ship needs only a little turn to change completely the
voyage and the destination. Often a minor change in husband-wife relationships can make a big difference.

Marriage Can Be Fun

G reg and Lisa had been married twenty-seven years. Friends who saw them together observed that they were always kidding around and seemed to be having a lot of fun. In reality they were! They went into marriage with an attitude of fun and maintained a light togetherness that seldom ebbed. How did they do it? Their goals for a great marriage included playing—regularly and often. Millions of couples miss the boat because they leave untapped the resources of play in marriage.

Psychiatrists and others advise that recreation is essential to the well-being of people. It is not only enjoyable, but also necessary for a balance in living. Couples who do not take time to play are cheating themselves; they are leaving untapped an excellent resource for building a positive marriage. Recreation can provide a re-creation of body and spirit, helping persons come alive and stay alive.

An elderly gentleman, the very picture of health, was asked by a friend how he managed to get along so well, maintaining his robust, charming self. The wise old man, past eighty-eight, replied, "I work hard and sit loose."

Some people overdo recreational aspects of living. A balance is needed: play should not be neglected, but it should not inundate the marriage either. In World War II, at the tragedy of Dunkirk and soon thereafter, the British agreed they would have to go all out to save themselves from invasion by Hitler. They went to a seventy-five-hour work week, closed many of the theaters, and announced that they had to work more and play less. Within a short time, it became evident that their goals were not being achieved—production sagged as recreation was curbed and the working week was overincreased. Reconsideration of the realities brought about a reduced working week, opening of the theaters, and restoration of many recreational facilities for the masses—and production went up.

Balance in living is analogous to a four-legged chair with its legs of work, rest, play, and worship. Each leg is essential, otherwise the chair tips over. If any leg is too long or fat, a similar instability may result. In other words, play and recreation are necessary in living, but there should not be too much of them. Some couples play too much, yet millions fail to enjoy each other and build their marriages through enjoyable recreational activities.

As well as being a personal release and a benefit to individuals, recreation between husband and wife can bring many positive effects: enjoyment, enrichment, and unifying of the team. Everybody wants to have fun in life; play between husband and wife can be a positive resource. Mates can get better acquainted, learn what brings joy and satisfaction to each other, and have their needs and wishes fulfilled. They also come closer to each other, more accessible. Spontaneity, creativity, and humor may abound. President David O. McKay said, "Every time a man laughs he takes a kink out of the chain of life."

Recreation can build and enrich a marriage. It can deepen relationships and divulge hidden parts of personality. It can build morale and increase understandings.

Play can be an integrating and unifying resource between husband and wife. Sharing their physical skills and abilities, as well as their minds in thinking and discussions, can weld a couple together in many ways. Husbands and wives who play tennis or golf or racquetball together are saying to each other, "You are important to me. I'll take time to be with you because you are high on my priority list." This is a powerful force for developing a feeling of belonging and for deepening the marital bond.

Marital partners do not have to be equal in skill to play together. They can test their skills and prowess with others of their own sex in addition to playing with each other.

Both physical and mental activities can help to strengthen and build a union between husband and wife. Reading the same book and discussing it, playing games, or writing histories can forge a team into a deepened oneness.

Husbands and wives who play together are also good therapeutically for each other. Play usually provides a physical release for tension and relaxes the participants—benefits that are essential for everyone. As one husband said, "I hit the tennis ball instead of people."

Couples need to develop their own patterns of play. Ideally, they will find recreational activities that are enjoyable for both. But a mature mate will also participate at times in a sport or activity that the partner really likes, whether that mate is eager about it or not. Again, playing involves giving as well as receiving.

For most couples a variety of activities seems to make sense, although they may well favor certain activities most of the time. Many couples find that intellectual pursuits can broaden their horizons while providing enjoyment together. These include such activities as taking classes together, joining discussion groups, or reading and discussing books together.

Couples can find many enjoyable activities that cost little or nothing: walking, hiking, camping, talking, playing house games, and participating in a whole gamut of sports, including tennis, racquetball, and swimming. Sometimes even cooking a meal together and preparing something different can be an exhilarating experience.

Not all recreation should be between husband and wife. Each needs to reach out past the marriage boundaries for associations and friendships. Men need recreation with other men, particularly in sports such as tennis, golf, or hunting; women need to associate with other women in similar activities, such as sports, women's organizations, and volunteer endeavors. From these outside activities mates can bring back news and impressions that can revive and enrich a marriage and add interest to daily routine.

Playing "with the boys" and "with the girls" should not be carried to the extreme. Some immature husbands and wives use outside recreation as a mechanism to escape from each other, which over a period of time may devastate a marriage. Moderation in play seems to be a sound rule.

Marriage can and should be fun. If it isn't, couples need to ask themselves: What's the matter with us? Do we think we are too busy? Aren't we capable of tapping recreational resources that are there for the asking? Are we not willing to give of ourselves for the benefit of each other and the marital team? Are we too serious? If couples are not having fun in marriage, they should sit down together and openly discuss where they want to go in regard to play and how to get there. If this doesn't bring the answer, they may well ask for counseling.

Teaming

*T*he story is told of a group of nineteenth-century pioneers crossing the plains to the West. At camp one evening two husbands were exchanging confidences about their wives. One said, "We get along fine." The other replied, "We don't get along at all," and added, "I wish we could get along like the two oxen pulling our covered wagon." "Yes," the first man retorted, "but they only have one tongue between them!"

Teamwork in marriage can make the difference. If a couple really work together and help each other, they have it made. If they don't, they are in trouble. As Lord Byron said, "All who joy would win, must share it—happiness was born a twin."

At the close of a lecture on marriage at a nondenominational church, a large woman, age eighty-six, sauntered to the front and approached the speaker, a sociologist and marriage counselor. He had talked about differing roles in marriage and had mentioned companionship in particular. The woman, when her turn came, observed in a soft voice, "That's what I have missed the most, being single all these years—companionship. I have yearned for someone to talk to, to listen to, even to differ with—but no person has been around!"

Counselors who talk to divorced people attest to the fact that a common regret of most divorcees is that there is no longer a team to belong to, a receptive companion to share and be with. Belonging and interacting, even though conflictive at times, are usually preferred to silence or emptiness.

On the positive side, synergy suggests that two or more persons can produce more at times by working together than they can by working individually and adding outputs. An interesting example of this proccess was the World Series of Mule Team Competition, held in Chicago in 1885. The winning team was able to pull 9,000 pounds, the second place team slightly less. Someone suggested combining the two teams—and together they were able to pull a 30,000-pound load.

Marital companionship provides fundamental needs of people, including (1) feelings of belonging, (2) opportunities to share thoughts and feelings, (3) a chance to help others, (4) a resource for receiving help when needed, and (5) opportunities for creating things together.

Marriage can provide a mutual sense of belonging that is unique—personal, intimate, private, and resentful of intrusion. "My mate belongs to me" and "We are on the same team" are powerful assertions in the lives of people. The need to belong is fundamental in human behavior; marriage opens the door for special intimate belongingness and oneness.

Marital companionship provides an opportunity for daily sharing of ideas and feelings, hopes and aspirations, as well as questions and failures. Sharing is so needed in the scheme of things. The team can provide a privacy and a support that is unknown to those who have not tied the marital knot. As one person said, "Home is the place where you can go when no one else will take you in."

The marital team provides a practical system for giving and getting help when needed. All people have problems and need assistance from others at times. Where better can a person go for help than to someone who loves and cares? Millions of husbands and wives affirm that their spouses have made a difference when the pathway has become rough or roadblocks have appeared. An understanding mate can listen and can help conflict or fearful vapors to disappear.

Ann, the wife of a graduate student, gave support in an

unusual but significant way. Her husband had difficulty one year with his eyes. She attended all his classes with him, took notes, and helped him understand them. She also read out loud to him each evening in their little apartment, with a curtain drawn between them so he could rest his eyes in the dark and she could have light to read. What a team!

A challenge always present for the marital team is to be creative. A husband and wife may plan, build, and furnish a house to make it, through their efforts, a customized home. They may grow vegetable and fruit gardens together; they may cook together; they may even do needlepoint together. And together they can create new life, one of the miracles of existence. They have the opportunity to join their hearts, their heads, and their hands in creating and doing.

Teamwork in marriage relates to the ways in which husband and wife treat each other and work together. Evelyn Duvall and Reuben Hill, in their book *When You Marry* (Boston: D.C. Heath and Co., 1953), describe five stages of social and emotional growth: receiving, manipulating, compromising, sharing, and creative cooperating. Newborn infants are entirely on the receiving end; if they don't get food, water, and warmth from others, they die. As children grow and mature, they learn that others play important roles in their lives, and that often they can control the behavior of others. They learn to cry in a certain way to get a certain response; they learn to manipulate mother or father or brother or sister to get what they want or need. As they mature still further, they learn that by compromising they can get what they want without depriving others. This stage can be illustrated by two little boys who want to play with the same fire engine at the same time. Their agreement to take turns works out satisfactorily for both.

Sharing is a more advanced stage, and can be illustrated by the same boys, with the owner of the fire engine saying to his friend, "Here, Mike, play with my engine for a while." There is no request or pressure here, but an open willingness to share the toy.

Creative cooperation, highest stage in the development of maturity and teamwork, involves doing things together, making things, and forging ahead from the known and usual to the new and different. One husband designed dresses for his wife to sew. Another couple planned and constructed an outdoor fireplace together, sharing the work. A young couple planned their own house and furnishings and did much of the painting and finishing work, sharing both the planning and the physical labor. Creative cooperation is an unselfish, giving, interlacing kind of activity that builds and enriches a marriage.

Marriages are in trouble when either or both mates operate mainly on the receiving and manipulation levels. A constant emphasis on getting and controlling brings problems. Mature partners are able to benefit from the resources and rewards belonging to compromise, sharing, and creative cooperation.

Authority is an important component of teamwork. Patterns for handling authority differ and should allow for individualities, but mature husbands and wives share most major decisions and many minor ones. On the other hand, mates should each have areas of their own in which they are most interested and most competent, and these jurisdictions should be respected. These areas should be decided by mutual consent.

Another approach to the team relationship is to think of three processes in interactions between people: dependence, independence, and interdependence. All these processes exist in all marriages, but the amount of each and the feelings of a couple toward them play significant roles in the well-being of mates.

Again, each infant comes into the world entirely helpless and dependent on others. Dependency exists as long as people live, but as they grow older maturity reduces the dependency. Usually growth moves in the direction of independence, which our culture stresses as a basic value, highly desirable. People who can think, feel, and act on their own are generally well respected.

Interdependence, in one sense the most mature stage of all, respects the reality of two or more people needing each other. Interdependent partners have their lives intertwined in many ways.

In a marriage, all three stages are important and

needed. It is only when dependence or independence is carried to the extreme that trouble erupts. At times husbands and wives need to be dependent on each other. They also often need to be independent, able to carry out individual responsibilities and decisions. Interdependence, a combination of dependence and independence, is essential for a team relationship. Fortunate are those couples who lean on each other at times, stand on their own feet often, and join their hands as well as their hearts at the right moments.

Opening Doors Through Appreciation

*M*argaret had been talking to her marriage counselor for nearly thirty minutes. Finally she broke down and said, with tears running down her cheeks, "If he'd only tell me that he loves me once in a while; if only he'd let me know that he appreciates what I do around the house. I can't stand dead silence." She went on to explain that her husband never gave her any words of endearment or thanks, and that she felt like an isolated, forgotten person on an island.

Showing appreciation is a vital part of successful marital living. It makes possible an enjoyable atmosphere and temperate emotional climate. It helps to smooth over the rough spots of stress and anxiety. As Mark Twain once said, "I can live for two months on a good compliment."

Educator John Dewey said, "The deepest urge in human nature is the desire to be important." Social psychologist W. I. Thomas suggested that there are four fundamental wishes shared by all people all over the world: the wish for security, the wish for new experience, the wish for response, and the wish for recognition. People need to be noticed, recognized, and appreciated. We are too apt to say, "She knows how much I think of her," instead of expressing this feeling to our loved ones. Even though we are aware the sun is shining somewhere, we still may shiver for lack of its glow and warmth.

In the marriage relationship, appreciation is particularly important because of the intimate life-style of husband and wife. It can enrich a relationship, smooth it, build it, and prevent problems from developing. For a marital partner to know that the other person notices and appreciates is essential to an endearing relationship.

Tevye, in the musical *Fiddler on the Roof,* asks Golde, time after time, "Do you love me?" She answers in song with the comment that after twenty-five years of her cooking his meals, cleaning his house, washing his clothes, and sharing his bed, he still asks, "Do you love me?" She hesitates to give a direct answer, but he asks again and again. Finally the positive response comes through, and the scene ends with the two sitting together, holding hands, singing, "It's nice to know."

Appreciation is a process of building and strengthening bridges between people. Nowhere is it needed more than between husbands and wives. Appreciation can lubricate the wheels of matrimony, bringing harmony, mutuality, and satisfaction.

Giving appreciation usually costs little or nothing, and can be done in a multitude of ways. Sometimes the most appropriate and eloquent expression is a simple and sincere thank you. Those two words said in the right tone of voice can be music to the marriage.

A few words from a husband, such as "That was well done," or "Your cookies are delicious," or "You look so nice and so does the house," make a difference. The wife who says "You look handsome tonight," or "Thanks for filling my car with gas," or "I appreciate your picking up the children," is strengthening the marital bond. Words of appreciation and endearment can change a humdrum marriage to one that is alive and warm. Affirmative communication is the essence of a vibrant relationship for both husband and wife.

Telephone calls are a practical, easy means of showing appreciation. A husband may call his wife and mention in the conversation what a fine breakfast he enjoyed with her. A thoughtful wife may telephone her husband and let him know how much she appreciated his surprise of doing the dishes before he left for work. All kinds of meaningful thanks can be conveyed through the remarkable wire of Alexander Graham Bell.

When husbands and wives are separated by trips, it is

important for them to keep in touch with each other; this provides them with the opportunity to show appreciation by telephoning or writing letters or both. One husband developed a pattern of calling his wife each evening when he was away from home. Often he not only told his wife he loved her, but also mentioned in sincere appreciation something specific she had done for or with him. A warm glow welled up within the hearts of both.

A physical, personal touch is powerful and intimate in expressing thanks and appreciation. A pat on the back, the shake of a hand, a wink of the eye, and, of course, hugs and kisses—all convey appreciation.

What about the frequency of appreciation? It should not be overdone or underdone. Showing too much appreciation makes it commonplace and monotonous. It lessens warmth and meaning. Showing too little leaves a mate hungering for something that is deserved and needed. If a couple have gone more than twenty-four hours without sharing their appreciation in some way, they are missing golden opportunities for building their marriage.

Variety in showing appreciation is desirable. Any action repeated too often may become dull and drab. Creativity and spontaneity are vital. A surprise note left on the dresser or in the briefcase, a special treat for dinner, tickets to a movie or show, or special words of endearment can bring joy and happiness to the recipient as well as the giver.

It is interesting to note that in showing appreciation, the giver is benefited as much as or more than the recipient. Edwin Markham describes it this way:

There's a destiny that makes us brothers;
　None goes his way alone:
All that we send into the lives of others
　Comes back into our own.

It is important not only *what* we say, but also *how* we say it. There is no room for sarcasm in mature husband-wife relations. Praise and thanks should be authentic, relevant, enthusiastic, and as specific as possible.

Building, Not Bruising

Scott and Barbara, married ten years, had had their ups and downs, but basically they shared a satisfying marriage with love deepening as the years went by. When differences or problems arose, they tried to help each other rather than bruise or batter one another. They were supportive and caring. When one did something the other didn't like, that person was so informed, not "battled" or "struck at." They recognized that all couples have many differences and problems, that the way to respond is to recognize that such problems exist and to face them, not to assert, "I'm right and you're wrong. I know what is best and you don't."

Just the opposite were Stephanie and Bob. They too had been married nearly ten years, but oh, what a marriage! When a conflict arose, each took a rigid position that he or she was right, and stuck to it. Psychological bruises appeared often. Their marriage was a spotty, difficult one; in fact, within another year they couldn't take it any longer, and they separated. No one can stand bruising or battering very long, whether it is physical or psychological. It hurts too much; the ego and body cannot take it.

Mature husbands and wives recognize that every person has both strengths and limitations that surface almost daily. They also recognize that stressing positive traits builds and strengthens a marriage, while focusing on limitations and mistakes tends to damage and destroy. Mates need to ask themselves: Which do I look at, strengths or shortcomings? Which do I emphasize most? Am I a builder or a destroyer?

Babe Ruth, baseball home run king, boasted a record of 715 home runs, an all-time high. People looked at his athletic record with awe and observed, "What a player! What a home run hitter!" It is interesting to note that Babe Ruth also went to bat and struck out more than thirteen hundred times. One can look at the life of Babe Ruth and say he was a great home run king, or emphasize the number of times he fanned out and say he was probably the greatest failure in baseball. Mates need to ask themselves: What do I do in my marriage?

Mature husbands and wives look at both the positives and the negatives in themselves, each other, and their marriage, but are accepting of the limitations and the mistakes made. They understand that the best way to bring change is by accepting, not battling—by focusing on positives. What is more important in marriage than this? Building each other results in achievement and accomplishments, physical and psychological. Bruising and battering hurt, and may reduce marriage to psychological rubble.

What can be done to build rather than to bruise or batter? Among other things, one can give deserved commendation, listen to what is being said, suggest alternatives, provide solace for failures, and give other support when needed.

Almost daily, husbands and wives can share sincere commendation for services performed or achievements reached. A sensitive husband tells his wife, "That cake is really delicious!" A mature wife tells her husband that the car he has just washed looks great, or that his fixing the light fixture is really appreciated. Each can give deserved praise for good deeds done.

Praise and commendation can be about little things as well as major accomplishments. The more specific the comment, the better. To say, "You gave a fine talk in church," is all right, but it is much better to say, "Your talk was especially effective because it reached the young people. I noticed they were listening intently."

Listening to both successes and failures is another way to build each other. As you hear and respond positively to your spouse's achievements, both of you feel good. When you listen to failures and fears in a reflective, understanding mood, you help build your mate and your marriage. Everyone needs a confidant to listen to negative feelings— feelings that often will disappear as they are talked out.

Another resource in building is to suggest alternative plans of action when questions and problems arise. An understanding mate can suggest different possibilities for solving a problem, giving the spouse more resources from which to choose.

Sympathetic marriage partners can build each other when each is in need of solace or genuine comfort. To have a mate say, even after a traumatic failure, "You can do it," really makes a difference and opens the door for another try. A depressed or discouraged partner is often helped by a spouse who listens and gives assurance that being "fed up" is normal at times and that things will likely be better soon.

Finally, mates can help by giving support for moving ahead and trying new things. A person who is hesitating on a business venture, in writing an article, or in considering asking for a raise may well receive encouragement from an understanding mate. He or she then moves ahead with added confidence rather than falling by the wayside. Goethe suggested, "If you treat a person as he is, he will remain as he is; if you treat him as he can and should become, he will become what he can and should become."

Positive building in a marriage strengthens and enriches the marital bond. President David O. McKay, at general conference, April 6, 1956, recommended "continued courtship" as contributive to a happy home, and then added: "Too many couples have come to the altar of marriage looking upon the marriage ceremony as the end of courtship instead of the beginning of an eternal courtship. . . . It is well to keep in mind that love can be starved to death as literally as the body that receives no sustenance. Love feeds upon kindness and courtesy. . . . The wedding ring gives no man the right to be cruel or inconsiderate, and no woman the right to be slovenly, cross, or disagreeable."

Dollars
and Sense

How much money is needed for a successful marriage? Most couples claim they do not have enough. There never seems to be an adequate amount even though the income may be substantial. Those with incomes below the poverty line often complain, justifiably so. Those with $40,000 yearly incomes say they have enough for the necessities but need more for the "niceties." Even millionaires claim they do not have adequate income to meet their needs. As incomes go up, needs and wants seem to go up faster. How important is money in marriage, and how should it be handled?

Three factors are important in handling finances: the amount of money available, the attitudes toward it, and the use of it. Most people seem to think the amount is most important, but experts claim that after you have enough for the necessities, the attitudes toward money and the use of it are most significant.

Economic factors are often a major problem in tottering marriages. Many husbands and wives complain about lack of money as one of their compelling difficulties. Lack of money is a debilitating factor for millions of persons and families. Even in the United States more than twenty-two million persons are living below the poverty line. On the other hand, most Americans have the minimum income necessary for food, clothing, and shelter.

Attitudes regarding money are particularly important. These involve feelings about its importance, desires to "keep up with the Joneses," and obtaining the numerous wants of husbands and wives. Mates can be accepting of their income or they can be critical of it. The importance of attitude is reflected in the account of the multimillionaire couple who committed suicide by sealing the cracks around the doors and windows in the kitchen of their commodious California home and turning on the gas stove. They left a note that read, "We have decided to do away with ourselves. We've had serious financial reverses. Life is not worth living." What they had lost was two million dollars, leaving only four million! They had luxurious homes in California and on the French Riviera, several automobiles, and all kinds of elaborate furnishings and belongings. But when they felt they had failed financially, that was the end.

Another example reflects entirely different money attitudes. A young couple with three small children moved from the South to work in the San Francisco shipyards. They lived in a slum area in a house with no lawns, part of a row of drab structures with no spaces between them. They had an old Cadillac, which they parked in front of the house, as a garage was not available. Yet, when interviewed, the husband and wife were happy and optimistic, and they observed that they were pleased about their economic situation. They were apparently well-adjusted, loving and caring for each other. Even though their circumstances were financially meager, they shared a harmonious marriage, and the family was joined together with feelings of love.

The use of money can make the difference between financial success or failure. For example, two married college students, each with two children, were enrolled in graduate school. The family incomes, through scholarships and part-time work, were about the same—nearly $9,000 a year. Although they both had to scrimp and be careful, they were able to obtain the basic necessities of life. Family A spent their money on some wasteful, unneeded things, and were constantly in dire financial straits. Couple B were careful with their income. They not only got along all right economically, but they also put a little money into savings, building for the future. One family was a failure financially, the other was making it all right—and the only difference was in how they used their income.

Family experts offer many suggestions for maintaining and building a family financially. Each family is unique and has to be flexible regarding its needs and wants, but the following are tested guidelines for married couples.

1. Careful planning is essential for adequate use of economic resources. This means a careful estimate and look at needs, wants, and sources of income. Either plan or perish. Instead of a hit-and-miss spending pattern, there should be careful anticipation of what lies ahead financially, and how the needs and wants can best be supplied.

2. Working out a specific budget is helpful. This is a specialized kind of planning. A budget contains specific listing of likely income and outgo within given periods of time. Most budgets are kept on a monthly basis, with anticipation of yearly needs. Allocations are included for food, clothing, housing, recreation, church and charity contributions, medical contingencies, and miscellaneous. A budget is a basic blueprint that can act as a guide; it may have to be altered on occasion for some unforeseen reason or development.

Husband and wife need to work out the budget together, or, at least, they both need to be aware of what it is and what it means. There are varying patterns for handling money; no one system is best for everyone. In one particular marriage a husband may administrate the family finances; in another, the wife may do it; or they may divide the responsibilities between them. Major expenditures should be agreed upon by both husband and wife. Each mate also needs some money for personal use without clearing with the other, so that both will feel a sense of independence. It is important that both partners feel comfortable with whatever system they ultimately choose.

3. Taking advantage of sales, seasonal and otherwise, may stretch the dollar. People who keep in touch with current prices can often purchase quality food and commodities at reduced rates. This requires a knowledge of specific brands and prices so that the savings are genuine.

Couples need to be careful not to buy unneeded items just because they are on sale. A buy is not a good buy, no matter what the price, if it is not needed and will never be used.

4. Ordinarily there should be an attempt to save some money as you go along. This can bring a sense of security as well as a nest egg for the future.

5. Secondhand objects and materials can be purchased to advantage at times. A used automobile can be an excellent buy and can save hundreds of dollars. Secondhand furniture or other items may fit the needs of a family at a given moment.

6. Most couples want to purchase a house. Care needs to be taken not to go into debt too steeply, but this is a good way to save over a period of years. Most economists suggest a couple should not invest more than two and a half to three times their annual income in a house.

Trust
Builds Trust

When couples join hearts and hopes at the marriage altar and say "I do," a private kingdom that resists intrusion is created. Here is a unique personal union that announces, "I'm yours and you are mine, and no one else's."

Although we live in a world with all kinds of people, many with contradictory moral values and behavior patterns, most adults in our society want a marital union that is sacred and private unto themselves. They do not condone seeking love and lovemaking outside the marital vows.

Trust engenders trust, while mistrust may result in wandering or going astray. Couples who really want the best in marriage maintain an abiding trust in each other.

Probably the two most important factors in the realm of trust are a sense of moral values and honesty. A couple who have faith in each other and possess these two factors have a decided asset for a successful marriage.

In the area of moral values, trust generates trust. If both husband and wife convey their confidence in each other's morality, they help build a relationship desired by both. When one or both begin to doubt and raise questions, trouble may ensue.

For example, Mr. and Mrs. Johnson, married thirty-one years, have complete confidence and trust in each other. They have been true to each other, and have sought variety and enrichment in life through and with each other rather than going elsewhere. They have built a private kingdom, unique and precious.

On the other hand, Mike and Cathy had been married twenty years when she began to accuse him of stepping out on her. Her charges were unfounded, but after awhile he started doing what she accused him of doing. The marriage went from bad to worse, and before long they separated.

Trust in marriage can help not only in maintaining the moral standards of the couple, but also in building and enriching their marriage. It can enhance the self-image and confidence of mates about themselves and their marriage. What is more powerful than the feeling that your mate knows that you will do what you've promised—that you will maintain your moral and ethical values? Trust builds confidence and deepens a marital bond.

Another important ingredient of success is for couples to share their basic values—preferably before marriage, but by all means in the early months of living together. This does not mean they can agree on every detail, but for a marriage to be a success, it is essential that there be a coming together of minds and feelings regarding what is of genuine value in life, including moral codes of living.

Honesty is another signal value. Telling the truth, as well as avoiding lies or false stories, is essential for harmonious marriage. Couples who do not tell the truth are in trouble. Dishonesty breeds contempt and multiplies dissent and conflict.

Honesty means telling the truth not only about major issues and situations, but about minor ones as well. This does not mean that mates have to share everything they think or feel or experience. Each person needs a private world of his own into which he may retreat if he feels the need. Also, at times a person may keep something confidential so it will not hurt the mate.

When questions are asked, honest answers should be given. If one mate cheats on the other, trouble will develop. There is no such thing as a secret—sooner or later the truth will come out. Sometimes a person has to be cruel in order to be kind; the sooner a difficult situation is shared, the better it usually turns out in the long run.

Bill and Rebecca, married twelve years, had been honest with each other and had a basically sound relationship. Then Bill began to gamble on the side. Soon he had lost all their money. He kept the secret to himself and the marriage began to falter. Rebecca sensed something was wrong. She kept asking Bill, "What's the matter?" He lied and said everything was all right. Finally he confessed the truth. It was difficult for her to accept, but accept the realities she did. They talked openly about the situation, and over a period of time, with the two of them working together with a marriage counselor, Bill was able to stop gambling. What happened to the marriage? Actually, the bond between them deepened as they faced their difficult situation together and honestly solved it.

Being married is more complicated than being single, but it also opens the door to experiences and enrichment in life that can be unique and wonderful. Couples who maintain a basic trust in each other, twenty-four hours a day, can build a kingdom of their own. Basic trust invites a constancy of thinking, feeling, and doing that makes life worth living. Mates who trust each other and are honest build each other as well as their marriage.

President David O. McKay echoes the same message: "Remember always that love is a tender flower, the roots of which are in the human heart. It thrives in the element of confidence and trust, as the rose thrives in the sunshine and morning dew. But in an atmosphere of mistrust, suspicion, or doubt of each other it will wilt, it will fade. Fidelity and constancy are to that little flower of the soul what the sun is to the rose." (*Home Memories of President David O. McKay,* p. 224.)

Spiritual Values

A poll of seven thousand students in twelve colleges revealed that only one percent of the students declared themselves to be atheists. Although many do not go to church, most Americans do belong to a church and millions do attend religious services. More significant than their church attendance is the underpinning belief in some kind of higher power that permeates their thinking and feeling. They have faith in something bigger and greater than themselves, and most attempt to tune in and be influenced by that power and belief. A recent sixty-nation survey, conducted by Gallup International and covering two-thirds of the world's population, reflected that ninety-four percent of the people in the United States "believe in God or a universal spirit."

The spiritual side of life is of paramount importance for most. Even those who do not possess religious beliefs themselves—atheists and agnostics—need to be aware of spiritual values and influences as they interact with others, especially with their wives or husbands.

Spirituality, which encompasses lofty values in the lives of people, is significant in marriage. It includes such values as worshipping, loving, giving, forgiving, and helping others. These values are significant in personality composition and in daily behavior. Spouses who agree on basic spiritual values have a decided advantage over those who differ.

Belief in a higher power and in spiritual values can strengthen a marriage; it can give purpose to life. Most youth and adults ask such fundamental questions as these: Who am I? Where did I come from? Where am I going? What is really important in life? Religious principles and sacraments help answer these questions and provide purposeful guidelines.

Psychologist T. H. Howells suggests that religion can provide meaning in life: "In a sense religious symbols are similar to the green flag which marks the location of the cup into which a golf ball is holed. Neither the cup nor the remote objectives of life are visible, but if the drives are directed toward the signs which symbolize them, one cannot go far wrong." (Quoted in D. B. Klein, *Mental Hygiene* [New York: Henry Holt and Co., 1944], p. 470.)

Most couples seek marriage within the same church, providing opportunities for worshipping together and for mutually tapping spiritual resources. Nevertheless, questions and problems often arise. Two people can belong to the same denomination and still share positive or negative feelings from this arrangement. Activity in the same church by both husband and wife is usually a solidifying factor; likewise, if they are both inactive, they may share a common understanding. If one is active and the other is not, trouble may appear. What will they do when the church representative comes to the door asking for a thousand-dollar contribution to build a chapel, or five hundred dollars to help with missionary work? The active person will likely say, "Let's do our share." The inactive mate may respond, "Let others do it. I don't think it's important."

If couples who belong to the same church differ on religious or spiritual values, what might they do? A first step is to talk over their differences. This might take several sessions, for religious values and feelings are usually deeply ingrained. In talking about differences, there needs to be an openness and sharing that is honest and kind. The aim is to bring into the open the genuine feelings and thoughts of both husband and wife. If mates honestly share what they think and feel, they can usually come to an understanding or agreement about where they are and where they should go. Solutions vary from couple to couple. One mate may become more involved in the religious activities of the other. They may both pull back from church activity. They may shift to another activity to replace church involvements, or they may agree to accept the fact that religion is one area in their marriage in which there are and likely will be differences.

Such acceptance may calm the troubled waters—until children come. Then there will need to be more talking and adjusting. Some parents say they'll let their children decide for themselves about religion. What this often means is that the children grow up with little or no religious inclinations or influences in their lives.

Another conflicting situation is when husband and wife belong to different denominations, and each believes that his or her religion is best. These differences should be talked over before marriage, but if they have not, or if intense feelings surface after marriage, careful consideration of these differences is necessary. Open communication may bring desired results—a coming together or some kind of compromise. It is essential that both husband and wife feel basically comfortable with the solution, which will vary from couple to couple.

If couples cannot work out a solution to spiritual differences, they may want to seek counseling. Religious conflict is a common problem brought to counselors, and they usually can be helpful. Some couples prefer to go to religious leaders in both churches to discuss their problems. Sometimes this can be helpful; other times it only complicates matters.

Latter-day Saints are encouraged to go to their bishop and talk over serious marital and family problems. Bishops are understanding, spiritual persons who often help couples directly or make it possible for them to utilize stake counseling resources or LDS Social Services. On the stake level many professional counselors volunteer to assist local members with individual or marital problems; on a churchwide basis LDS Social Service agencies dot the United States and are found in many foreign countries. These agencies are staffed by professionally trained workers who are also spiritually resourceful.

Spiritual values can be definite assets to a marriage. Brief consideration of a few values that inhere in spiritual codes illustrates their importance. These include loving, giving, and forgiving. As mentioned earlier, the greatest need in this world is for people to love and be loved, to care for and be cared for. Religions stress that loving is the greatest commandment of God, that it is the essence of successful daily living. Church leaders are constantly teaching and preaching about the efficacy of loving. Knowing about love is not enough; loving is the test.

Giving is advocated and stressed by all religions and in all churches. The idea proclaimed is that people are on earth with the challenge and opportunity to help others and, in so doing, to help themselves. The basic teaching is encompassed in the Golden Rule: "Do unto others as you would have them do unto you." Couples who adhere to this dynamic teaching find that their marriages deepen and become even more meaningful. The pages of history reflect that as people give of themselves and their time, they benefit others, themselves, and their marital relationships.

Religions teach that we should forgive one another of mistakes and shortcomings. As husbands and wives practice this principle, they strengthen their relationships and bring harmony to their marriages. A forgiving person can help build the mate and the marriage by having an accepting attitude, allowing for new beginnings. Since we all make mistakes, it should be easy for us to forgive one another.

Parenting

*H*ow important is it to be a parent? In this jet-propelled world of speed, synthetics, and scientific marvels, ideas and opinions differ and change as never before in the history of mankind. Answers vary from "being a parent is the greatest opportunity in life," to "parenting is not for me."

The reality is that most people who marry hope for and plan for children. Many desire two or three; others want many more. For most married persons, parenthood is one of the greatest goals in life.

What does effective parenting involve? Sound parenting does not just happen; it takes understanding, time, and effort. Certain guidelines can assist couples in this challenging calling.

First is the importance of loving. The greatest need of children is to be loved and to love. To care for others and be loved unconditionally in return is the essence of living. The essential nature of it is illustrated by the account of divorce proceedings involving a family with an eight-year-old daughter and a five-year-old son. The judge called the little girl into his private chambers and asked her preference as to whom she would prefer to go with, her mother or her father. She answered, "I love them both and can't say." Then she pleaded, "Whatever you do, judge, don't separate me from my brother; he needs me."

Loving involves affection, acceptance, giving of time and self, sacrifice, building, commendation, and other positive actions. Since love is so important, it is essential to let each child know he or she is loved, regardless of what each does. You can still love your children even though you hate some of the things they do. There is a big difference between criticizing a child for what he has done and finding fault with what he is. Most children can take questioning about their behavior, but they become emotionally disturbed when questions are aimed at their worth as persons.

During World War II when bombs were obliterating parts of London, Rotterdam, and other cities in Europe, many children were evacuated from populous centers, which were the major targets. Many of the children were removed from their parents and placed in homes in the countryside. Studies later divulged some interesting results: they showed that children who were removed from their parents became more upset and had more problems than did those who stayed with their parents, even in the midst of the bombings. In other words, the love and security of being with the parents was more significant than being out of reach of devastating explosives. The importance of love in the growth and development of children was reaffirmed.

Children can bring both joy and problems to a home— in fact, they usually do bring both. Most parents look forward with great anticipation and are filled with joy when the newborn infant arrives. Their happiness is sublime. Such feelings may exist as long as they live. On the other hand, the day the newborn infant enters the family he or she also brings complications. Time must be allocated for the new infant as well as for the other children and the spouse. There are economic adjustments, social adjustments, eating adjustments, and other changes that affect the climate and disturb established patterns of family living. Wise parents realize that children will bring both happiness and challenges, and they adjust accordingly.

The attitudes of a couple toward having children are important. The more positive they are, the more successful their parenting is likely to be. Parents who have negative attitudes toward having children may inflict indelible negative influences on them from the day of birth.

It is desirable to develop positive, realistic attitudes in the other children prior to the infant's arrival. Young children, as well as older ones, have ambivalent feelings about any new addition to the family. For example, in a family with two girls, ages three and five, the three-year-old was positive most of the time about the prospect of a new baby in the family. However, when she went with her grandparents to the hospital, she commented, "We are going to the hospital to get my mother, and we'll leave the baby there." Soon she voiced the opposite, "It will be fun to have a baby brother." Children vacillate just as parents do. Ambivalent feelings are normal, even in relation to someone we love.

Husbands and wives need to plan for the baby, share how they feel about it, and discuss what they need to do to prepare for it. The new arrival introduces a family triangle. Regardless of a couple's preparation and mature feelings, the marriage will never be the same. As they talk over the impending birth, they can raise and discuss their questions, anticipate what needs to be done, and recognize that their lives will be different. All this requires maturity as never before; parenthood is definitely for grown-ups.

The essence of loving and caring is illustrated by the family whose three-year-old daughter was sleeping in a room adjoining that of her parents. Once she awakened at about two A.M. and called for a drink of water. Her father got out of bed and gave her a drink. Wide awake by then, she began talking and singing and disturbing the whole house. Finally the father went to the side of her bed and said softly, "Everyone is asleep. You'll have to be quiet, honey." For a few moments there was silence; then a little voice called out, "Daddy, is your face turned toward mine?" The father was awake enough to answer, "Yes, Becky." She replied, "All right, I can go to sleep then," and within seconds she was off to dreamland.

Wise parents spend time with their children, individually and together. It is very important that a child feel that his parents care enough about him to be with him. Parents who seldom take time for their children are cheating both the children and themselves. Even the busiest parents can take time to be with their family if they really want to. One father, away from home on business most of the time, would spend a minimum of two hours with each of his four children each time he was in town, with the open invitation to do whatever the child chose. This was a powerful manifestation of caring.

It is important for children to know that they are accepted and that they belong to the family regardless of what they do. Children need walls around them; they need security-giving discipline. The child who is left alone to do just what he wants will come, sooner or later, to resent his parents. He will feel that his parents don't care enough about him to give directions or to tell him what to do and what not to do. Psychiatrists emphasize that children need discipline and restrictions just as they need love. Wise parents work out a sound and fair system of discipline and adhere to it. They do not overdo it or become unduly upset when misbehavior results. They know that no child is perfect. They are accepting and understanding, but they may also place a child in his room for a while as a means of punishment, if needed. Physical punishment is not generally advised; there are other, more effective ways of dealing with misbehavior, such as an isolation period, or having a special privilege denied for a set period of time. Some useful guidelines for discipline of children are these:

1. Discipline should be as close as possible to the misdeed. The mother should refrain from saying, "Just wait until your father gets home!" She should deal with the misbehavior when it occurs.

2. Guidance should be shared by both husband and wife.

3. Many trivialities should be overlooked.

4. Consistency is particularly important.

5. The certainty of discipline is usually more important than the severity.

6. Discipline should be individualized.

7. The best discipline is preventive guidance.

Consistency of parents is essential at all times. Parents also need to be consistent between themselves. For a father to say one thing and the mother to say the opposite brings confusion and mistrust. Also, for either to say and do one thing at seven A.M. and the opposite at seven P.M. doesn't make sense to a child.

The importance of consistency is illustrated by a study

with rats. The researchers conditioned the behavior of the rats by showing a white square card and giving them food as a reward for going up an incline and jumping to a box. After a while the rats would jump when the white square was shown alone. The scientists also conditioned the same rats to come up the incline and not jump when they were shown a red circle cardboard. The researchers then played a trick on the rats. Both the white square and the red circle cards were flashed, alternately, close together. The rats didn't know what to do. They received the signal to jump and then the signal not to jump. Becoming confused, they turned over on their backs and kicked their feet in the air. They had to be taken to the "rat hospital." Children are not so different when they get conflicting messages or signals from parents.

Parents need to spend time talking with their children about the facts of life, whenever questions arise and as the children grow up. Parents should use the proper names of personal parts of the body and not shame or embarrass their children when they ask questions. It is not a question of whether or not children are going to get sex information; it is only a question of where they will get it. Ordinarily, parents can do a better job of educating their children about sex than can the children's peers on the school playground. Parents need to be honest, open, and interested in helping their children gain a factual understanding of the reproductive process and of lovemaking, with the information they give being appropriate for the children's age and maturity.

Some parents give too much personal information too fast. Middle ground in this area, as in others, seems to make sense. As one psychiatrist said, "You don't set a child up in the lumber business just because the child asks a question about a tree in the forest."

Parents need to give their children gentle pushes away from them so they gradually become independent and responsible. Actually, the best way to keep children close is to push them gently away. Too many parents carry their children around for years, then wonder why they cannot stand on their own feet.

One psychiatrist described the process of developing

responsibility in a child by using the analogy of a fence around a child. At first, the fence is close, firm, and enveloping; then gradually it can and should be moved outward so the child has more opportunity to learn and to manage on his own. As parents, with gentle pushes, gradually move the fences of protection and security, the child replaces excessive dependency with an independent and interdependent maturity. Some parents hold their children too tight and too long; others remove or shift the fences and supports too soon and the children are overwhelmed. A proper balance between protection and freedom nurtures a child into maturity. The embroidered picture framed on the wall reaffirms the same idea: "There are only two lasting gifts we can give to our children—one is roots, the other wings."

Counseling Resources

*I*f something goes wrong with your car, you may find a service station, or two or three, on a nearby intersection. If your marriage backfires, where can you go? Should you talk to a friend or a relative? Who is most likely to help? Should you search the yellow pages in the telephone book for a marriage counselor?

Marriage counselors are available in populous cities and in many other areas. (A few years ago a new Miami Beach hotel announced it had hired a marriage counselor to be at the disposal of honeymooning guests.) However, some persons may have to travel quite a distance to reach a competent counselor. The American Association for Marriage and Family Therapy, a professional group that maintains standards and helps protect the public from quacks, provides names and addresses of competent counselors.

Care should be taken to find out about a counselor before going to him. It is estimated there are more than 25,000 quacks doing personal and marital counseling in the United States, milking the public of at least $500,000,000 annually. The money is incidental to the damage that may be caused in the personal and family lives of persons who get caught in their clutches. The safest procedure is to go to someone who is known personally or recommended by a friend or professional associate.

Is there a need for marriage counseling? Most people agree that the family is still the basic institution of society, and many religions proclaim it as the basic unit in the kingdom of God. Yet it is clearly evident that the family is in trouble, and that millions of men, women, and children are affected each year by family dissensions and breakups. In recent years the divorce rate has been spiraling; in 1975, for the first time more than 1,000,000 divorces were granted in the United States. This meant that more than 3,000,000 men, women, and children were influenced by formal family separations. Each divorce is symptomatic of trouble, and each creates problems for all involved.

In addition to this, thousands of families are broken annually by desertion, usually involving the husband's leaving home, saying he won't be back. Now we also have runaway wives who desert their homes and families. And in addition to divorce and desertion, many couples just separate, each going his or her own way. *All* couples have problems, in varying degrees, and many successful marriages occasionally need temporary or sustained help to weather marital storms. Marriage counselors today are also helping with marriage enrichment for successful marriages, making them more enjoyable. Why not?

Most couples do not need to go to marriage counselors. Even though they may have differences and problems, most can and should work them out by themselves. They can sit down with each other, share their feelings and problems with honesty and kindness, recognize that all couples have problems, and help each other handle conflicting situations. When a couple really share their own needs, feelings, and desires with each other, accepting each other completely, and honestly and fairly trying to help each other, their marriage usually will take a turn for the better. Conflicts may help build a marriage and the relationship *if* the mates are willing to really listen and help each other. If the differences or problems are serious enough, or if they keep recurring frequently, the path to a qualified marriage counselor may well be followed.

Most people harbor fears about going to a marriage counselor. They hesitate to share personal feelings, to admit that they have made mistakes and that their marriage has imperfections in it. When they once recognize that they are not unusual, that no marriage is perfect, they can begin to change. It should be understood that marriage counselors keep all that they hear strictly confidential.

They also have already heard just about everything that could happen, and will not be embarrassed, no matter what is brought up. Their only aim is to help persons and couples think and feel through what their needs are and learn how best to attain them.

The process and meaning of marriage counseling was depicted by a client who said, "It is like looking in a mirror for the first time. I never really saw, heard, or felt myself before. It hurt, but it was also a great relief. It is hard for me to tell you how I feel about it, but it seemed to me that I was receiving love, not personal, but all-understanding."

Qualified counselors do not tell a couple what to do; they help them to help themselves. As stated by Michael Drury, popular author on marriage, a marriage counselor "acts as a kind of big canvas on which you paint a picture of your situation; then you can stand back and take a good look. With *your* efforts, he helps you make an adjustment. He never makes it for you."

The goal of marriage counseling is to help a couple look at themselves and their problems realistically, to help them view alternative plans of action, and to be supportive of that which they choose to do. The counselor does not make decisions for the couple; rather, he helps them muster their resources and make their own decisions, depending on their thoughts and feelings about what seems best. All sharing and reflecting is done on a confidential basis so no one knows about it except the couple—no gossip, no rumors, no innuendos.

What are the main services provided by marriage counselors? Six are described briefly here.

1. *Provide information.* No couple or person has full knowledge or complete understanding about actions and reactions involved in marriage. Counselors can share selected readings and knowledge on such subjects as love-making, budgeting, child rearing, recreational pursuits, or religious practices. As the couple increase their knowledge in areas in which they have conflicts, they are usually able to reduce their problems.

2. *Allow for ventilation of feelings.* Everyone has had the experience of being vitally concerned or fearfully anxious about a problem or situation, only to have it

diminish or evaporate through someone's listening to a description of it. A major role of marriage counselors is to listen sympathetically and to allow for vaporization of concerns, fears, doubts, or even hates.

3. *Help in decision-making.* All couples have difficulties in making decisions, some more than others. Some become bogged down by indecision and are unable to cope with alternatives facing them. Again, the marriage counselor does not make decisions for the couple, but helps them consider alternatives and select their own choices.

4. *Help to define the situation.* Making decisions involves thinking and rationality, a process that relates in particular to feelings. One couple, childless for ten years and wanting children, might approach a counselor with the husband saying, "We want to adopt a child," and the wife adding, "I want to, but I wonder if I could do a good job of rearing someone else's baby." The counselor can help them express their feelings and move in the direction they really want to go.

5. *Assist in the reorganizing of behavior patterns.* In one sense this is the most difficult process of all. It has to do with such deep behavior problems as alcoholism, homosexuality, or drug abuse. Nevertheless, marriage counselors describe all kinds of marital problems involving these kinds of situations that have been aided through counseling.

6. *Make referrals.* A major difference between a professional marriage counselor and a quack is that the quack wants to hang on to his clients as long as possible, to keep the money flowing into his pockets; the professional aims to have the client stop coming as soon as it is possible. He will be the first to refer the client to another person if this seems appropriate. Referral might be made to a psychiatrist if deep emotional problems exist, to a minister for spiritual guidance, to a geneticist for questions about heredity, to a lawyer for legal counsel, or to a banker or financial adviser for financial assistance.

Latter-day Saints are encouraged to go to their bishop if they have difficult individual, marital, or family problems. Bishops can be most helpful in regard to these matters as well as counsel about spiritual situations. If further assistance is needed, referral can be made to the stake president, who can make stake resources available. Many Church members with professional training and skills have volunteered their services to help members with personal and marital problems. If additional assistance is needed, priesthood leaders can refer a member or family to LDS Social Services, which provides counseling by qualified social workers, psychologists, psychiatrists, and others with special training. LDS Social Service agencies are available in many parts of the United States and in several other countries. They provide consultation, evaluation, and training for priesthood leaders as well as marriage counseling, on a short-term basis, for individuals and families.

Courting couples and married couples need to keep in mind that marriage and other counselors are available if serious problems arise and persist. Counselors do not have all the answers, but they are able to help with most problems, and can make referrals to others when appropriate.

Looking Ahead

W hat about the future? If you could look into a crystal ball and see what is ahead, life would take on many different meanings. The realistic alternative is to anticipate likely possibilities and then plan and hope for the best.

Life ahead is uncertain. We all face unknown situations, challenges, and opportunities. Changes are inevitable in marriage, and flexibility and adaptability are essential. Your marriage will never again be the same as it is today.

Alvin Toffler, in his book *Future Shock* (New York: Random House, 1970), notes that the shock of change affects every person and every marriage. He suggests: "The flood of novelty about to crash down upon us will spread from universities and research centers to factories and offices, from the marketplace and mass media into our social relationships, from the community into the home. Penetrating deep into our private lives, it will place absolutely unprecedented strains on the family itself."

Nothing stands still in human relations. Changes bring alterations in living, and sooner or later they may bring crises. In marriage, changes and crises can bring difficulties, opportunities for growth, or both.

Two mature persons can face uncertainties together better than they can face them alone. Sharing fears, anxieties, and doubts is a positive experience. Husbands and wives can bolster each other in times of crisis or uncertainty.

Certain patterns of behavior are important in moving

into the years ahead. First is a realistic acceptance that change is certain. There is no way that life can go on exactly as it has in the past. One of the certainties of life is the constancy of uncertainty; change is inevitable. Mature husbands and wives understand that the days ahead will be different. They maintain their values and behavior patterns from the past, but are flexible as they go around the corners.

Second, mature mates maintain a balance in living, gaining satisfaction mainly from the now, not the past or future. Joy and satisfaction inhere in the now. The present is the time for enjoyment and zestful living. When tomorrow arrives, it becomes the today of importance.

The present moment is the one that is alive and vibrant. In beautiful Forest Park in St. Louis, Missouri, is a large floral clock that tells the time to those who pass that way. Attractive plants add beauty and warmth to the big hands as they move around slowly. At the bottom of this picturesque slope are the words, spelled in green foliage, "Hours and flowers soon fade away." Husband and wife may well absorb some of the philosophy contained in this statement and recognize that each hour of the present is a golden opportunity.

The words "Do It Now" are particularly important in the marriage endeavor. Postponement and procrastination may corrode a relationship and bring a marriage to the brink of disaster. Achievement and satisfaction come from *doing*. The essence of satisfaction inheres in asking, "What would be the best thing for me to do right now?"—and then in doing it.

Mature mates recall the past to enhance their perspective and to add color to the present, and they look to the future with hope and optimism. But they dwell mostly in the present, realizing that today offers inner joy and contentment.

Faith in oneself, in one's mate, and in marriage is essential for successful living. It brings confidence and a feeling of being able to do and to share, to taste of life to the fullest. Everyone has feelings of inferiority and inadequacy at times, but persons who accept themselves as they are, with confidence and self-caring, are the ones who move into the future in a positive way.

In some ways, faith and confidence in one's mate are even more important than self-esteem and self-confidence. To know that one's mate really cares about and believes in one can often make the difference. The feeling that "my partner knows *I Can Do It*" can help one open the door to action with confidence and feelings of achievement.

Faith in the future and preparation for the times ahead are imperative if we are to have joyful living in the present. The importance of faith is illustrated by the account of the five-year-old girl who, in 1885, took her first trip by horse and buggy from her home in a small farming village. She was accompanied by her father, who told her they would follow a picturesque canyon road to a city thirteen miles away. As the buggy bumped along the narrow road, hugging the splashing stream in many places, the girl noticed that the walls of the canyon were narrowing. Fear began to rise within her. Soon, as she looked ahead, she could see only massive rocks and huge cliffs apparently blocking the way. Rain began to fall, and the girl cried, "We'll never make it. I want to go home." Her father put his arm around her and reassuringly said, "Honey, we'll make it all right. We'll just follow the road." And follow the road they did. Soon the dark clouds disappeared, the canyon walls widened, and before long the big city was before them. Somewhat similarly, as couples have faith in each other and follow their marital goals, they realize that, come what may, everything will work out all right.

Planning is essential if a couple are to meet the future. Planning involves both short-range and long-range goals; every marital team needs both. Planning varies from couple to couple, but a pattern that is comfortable to both partners is needed. Both individual and team planning are important on a regular basis, sometimes daily, other times weekly or monthly. Many couples take a careful look at themselves and their marriage at the beginning of each year.

Short-range planning is essential. Individuals and couples should work out their own patterns for formulating goals and plans. A small notepad provides an easy, economical way. Each morning write on the pad the things you want and need to do that day. Set them in order of priority, and start with number one. Ordinarily you will not achieve all you set out to do, but you will probably accomplish much. People who have specific targets in focus are more likely to achieve objectives than those who are floating with the breezes without any directions in mind.

Goal setting should be specific, not general. For example, a couple may say, "We want to go out together once a week," and follow this schedule. This would be better than saying, "Let's have more fun together by going out more often." Being specific is essential in goal setting and planning.

Long-range planning is also needed. Goals that are set and then reviewed occasionally provide fertile guidelines for a couple to establish short-range targets. Wise husbands and wives sit down together every now and then and ask themselves: Where are we? Where are we going? Where do we want to go? How do we get there? They then blueprint their specific targets for the present and future.

It is important to consider both wants and needs. Couples are entitled to look for and move toward what they *want* in life. This is normal and desirable. However, people must consider that they and others have *needs* as well. A blending of planning for *wants* and *needs* is fundamental for successful marriage.

It is also essential that a couple share the desire and action needed to enrich their lives. Monotony and boredom may ruin a relationship. New experiences and surprises brighten and enrich a marriage, bringing zest and meaning. Mates who each day reach outward, upward, and onward, and who desire to have new experiences are those who really taste of life.

New experiences need not be costly; many that bring deep satisfaction are free. A walk in the park or around the block in the evening, a trip to a different eating place, a visit to a friend in need or to someone who is not expecting you, the creation of new things for the house or yard— these and numerous other experiences can bring life and joy to a world filled with uncertainty.

"We are all functioning at a small fraction of our capacity to live fully in its total meaning of loving, caring, creating, and adventuring," says Herbert Otto, well-known marriage counselor. "Consequently, the actualizing of our potential can become the most exciting adventure of our lifetime."

In the end, the essence of living successfully each day, of moving into the future with confidence and vitality, is what we do *for* and *with* each other. The genius of spirited living is giving of ourself for our mate and our marriage. As two people give *to, for,* and *with* each other, they walk on the path to happiness.

The present and future are right for you if you will use your head, your heart, and your hands for your mate and your marriage. This means, of course, that you will think and act positively and will harmonize your feelings. Combining marital thinking, feeling, and doing opens the door to a great marriage—which can become much more than a dream. Do *you* want it?

Index

Acceptance: of mate, 35-38; children need, 75

Accident in automobile following argument, 2

Achievements of mate, gaining satisfaction from, 11

Actions: effect of, on marriage, 3-4; involved in nurturing love, 21

Affection: importance of showing, 22-23; physical, in marriage, 23-25

Alcoholic husband, wife who showed acceptance of, 36-37

Anger, dealing with, 12-13

Appreciation, importance of showing, 55-57

Arguments in marriage, 2; resulting from differing expectations, 5. See also Conflicts in marriage

Attitudes, proper: importance of, in marriage, 3; in communication, 16; regarding finances, 61-62; developing, in older children when new baby comes, 73-74

Authority, areas of, 53

Babe Ruth, 59

Balance in living, 47, 84

Behavior patterns, 81, 84

Belonging, sense of, 51

Bishops, counseling role of, 70, 81-82

Bombings, evacuating children away from, 73

Bruising and battering, 58

Budgeting, 63

Building one another, 58-59

Chair, four-legged, analogy of, 47

Change, inevitability of, 83-84

Children: effect of, upon marriage, 73; ambivalent feelings of, toward new babies, 74; parents should spend time with, 74-75; disciplining, 75; teaching, about facts of life, 76

Commendation, 59

Communication: presents greatest problems in marriage, 14; two components of, 14-15; verbal and nonverbal, 15; clarity in, 16; feedback in, 17; requires honesty and kindness, 18; over religious conflicts, 69-70

Companionship, 50

Competition in marriage, 11

Compromises, making, 43

Confidences, importance of keeping, 16-17

Conflicts in marriage: dealing with, 12-13; inevitability of, 42-43; over religious differences, 69-70

Consistency in discipline, 75-76

Counseling, professional, 44-45, 70, 78-79, 80-81

Courtship, continuing, after marriage, 60

Creative cooperation, 52-53

Decision making, 81

Demanding too much, 7

Dependency, 53

Discipline, children need, 75

Divorce, statistics concerning, 1, 79

"Do It Now" attitude, 84

Dreaming about marriage, 1

Expectations: differing, 5;

everyone has, about
marriage, 6; solving
differences in, 7;
understanding one another's,
is important to marriage, 8

Facts of life, explaining, to
children, 76
Faith in self and mate, 84-85
Family ties, 37
Feedback in communication, 17
Feelings: often control
behavior, 3, 9; vacillate up
and down, 9-10, 36; real,
failure to recognize, 10;
sharing, with mate, 10-11;
pent-up, need to release, 17,
80-81; negative, should be
shared, 18; ability to
recognize, in mate, 28-29
Fiddler on the Roof, 56
Fifty-fifty proposition, marriage
is not, 32
Financial resources: sharing, in
marriage, 34; attitudes
toward, 61-62; use of, 62-63
Forgiveness, offering, 41, 71
Future, preparing to face, 83

Gambling, husband's problem
with, 66-67
Giving: love involves, 21-22,
importance of, in marriage,
31; of total self, 32
Goals, 85-86
God, widespread belief in, 68
Goethe, 60
Golden Rule, 71

Happiness, 9; marrying to gain,
31; was born a twin, 50
Help, giving and getting, 51
Honesty, 66
House, purchasing, 64
Humor, sense of, 13

Ice cream, throwing, 13
Imperfections, everyone has, 36
Independence, 53-54; helping
children develop, 76-77

In-laws, 37
Interdependence, 53-54

Judging, 35-36

Laundry, argument over, 5
LDS Social Services, 45, 70, 82
Likes and dislikes: about
spouses, 12; about self, 28
Listening, 11; with heart as well
as ears, 15; importance of, in
good communication, 16; to
both successes and failures,
59-60
Love: importance of, to life, 19;
definitions of, 19-20;
marriage offers greatest
opportunities for, 20;
mature, vs. childish, 20; is
constantly changing, 20-21;
actions involved in, 21; must
have nourishment, 25;
thrives on trust, 67;
emphasis given to, by most
religions, 70-71; importance
of, in parenthood, 72-73

Manipulation, 52-53
Marriage: statistics concerning,
1; pressures of, 2; is journey,
not destination, 2-3;
expectations concerning, 5-8;
is team effort, not
competition, 11; offers
greatest opportunities for
loving, 20; physical relations
in, 23-25; relationship of,
requires nourishment, 25-26;
importance of giving to, 31;
is not a fifty-fifty
proposition, 32; conflict is
normal in, 42-43; should be
fun, 46-49; teamwork in, 50;
showing appreciation is vital
to, 55-57; creates a private
kingdom, 65; interfaith, 69-
70; effect of children upon,
73; building a great, 87
Marriage counselors, 44-45, 70,
78-79; services provided by,
80-81

Maturity: in love, 20; in handling mistakes, 40-41; different stages of, 52; parenthood requires, 74; nurturing children into, 77

McKay, David O., 47, 60, 67

Millionaires who committed suicide, 62

Mirages, 10

Mistakes: admitting, 28, 40; lying about, 39; accusing others for one's own, 40; maturity in handling, 40-41

Monotony, overcoming, 86

Mountain peaks, relative size of, 6-7

Mule team competition, 51

Needs, fundamental, 51, 55; providing for, 86

Negative feelings, sharing, 18, 60

Newton, Isaac, 14

Nonverbal communication, 15

Old Faithful, 18

Parents: planning to become, 72; must have great love, 72-73; should spend time with children, 74-75

Perspective: differences in, 6-7; spouse's, seeing things from, 29

Physical relations in marriage, 23-25

Planning: financial, 63; short- and long-range, 85-86

Playing, resources of, 46-49

Positive traits, focusing on, 58-59

Praise, specific, 59

Present, dwelling in, 84

Priorities, setting, 33

Privacy of marital union, 65

Problem solving, suggesting various possibilities for, 60

Rats, experiment with, regarding consistency, 76

Realistic attitudes, 29

Recreation, role of, in marriage, 46-49

Relatives, influence of, 37

Religious beliefs: most Americans possess, 68; answer fundamental questions, 68-69; provide direction in life, 69; marital conflicts over, 69-70

Responsibility, helping children develop, 76-77

Sacrificing, love involves, 22

Sales, taking advantage of, 63-64

Self: learning to understand, 28; is easiest person to change, 29, 36

Selfishness, 32

Sex education, 76

Sexual relations in marriage, 23-25

Sharing: of time, talents, and money, 33-34; stage of, in social growth, 52

Spirituality in marriage, 68

Supporting attitudes, 11, 51-52, 60

Talents, sharing, 33-34

Talking *with* rather than *to* each other, 15-16

Teamwork in marriage, 50, 52

Time: giving, to spouse, 32-33; spending, with children, 74-75

Trust: generates trust, 65; effect of, on marriage, 66-67

Twain, Mark, 55

Understanding: is major factor in marriage, 28; of self, 28; of mate, 28-29; lack of, may produce conflict, 43

Values: understanding one another's, 8, 66; religious, 69-70

World War II, 46-47, 73